An Antidote Against Arminianism
OR
A TREATISE TO ENERVATE AND CONFUTE
ALL THE FIVE POINTS THEREOF;

Viz.:
Predestination Grounded upon Man's Foreseen Works
Universal Redemption
Sufficient Grace in All
The Power of Man's "Free Will" in Conversion
The Possibility of True Saints Falling Away Totally and
Finally

Recommended by John Owen

Written by CHRISTOPHER NESS
(LONDON: FIRST PRINTED IN THE YEAR 1700)
With extracts from John Gill, Isaac Watts,
Augustus Toplady, John Newton and J. Hart

STILL WATERS REVIVAL BOOKS
12810-126ST. EDMONTON, AB., CANADA T5L 0Y1
"PUBLISHING THE TRUE PEACE" (Isa. 52:7)

* * *
"For **free** information regarding this and other Christian
topics, (such as a list of free Christian newsletters and how
to get the best prices on Christian literature, music and
Bibles); send a self addressed stamped envelope to the
publisher.
* * *

Printed in the United States of America
1988
Deluxe Edition   ISBN 0-921148-02-X

CONTENTS

CHAPTER I.
OF PREDESTINATION.

CHAPTER II.
OF UNIVERSAL REDEMPTION.

CHAPTER III.
OF FREE WILL AND CONVERSION

CHAPTER IV.
OF FINAL PERSEVERANCE.

AN INTRODUCTORY PARABLE

"So is the potter sitting at his work, and turning the wheel about with his feet, who is always anxiously set at his work, and all his handiwork is by number; he will fashion the clay with his arm, and he will bend it's strength in front of his feet; he will apply his heart to finish the glazing; and will be wakeful to make clean the furnace" (Ecclesiasticus 38:39, 30).

The constantly spinning wheels of the potters trade in the ancient East produced vessels of clay for many purposes. The wealth of a household could be determined by the multitude, variety and quality of dishes, pots, urns and jars. "In a great house are many vessels, some to honour and some to dishonour" (II Timothy 2:20).

The potter often prepared a heavy cone-shaped lump of clay and carefully centred it on his rotating wheel, so that this lump came up to a soft, moist point. Then, with his wet hands he would press and slide up the sides of the spinning lump, while pressing down on the point with his thumbs at the right moment, with just the right pressure, delicately to shape the jar. Then, with a wire or a sharp piece of wood he would cut this newly formed vessel from the top of the cone and place it on his protected bench or shelf to dry. Now a delicate jar could dry too quickly or unevenly and crack, so the potter might wet his hands and soon form another jar of uniform thickness from the same spinning lump. This second one he would make large enough to place over and cover the first jar. When he had severed it from the top of that lump, he would turn it upside down, and carefully lower it, so that the first jar would be inside the second. After the two jars had dried slowly together, he would display the first one and use the second for a disposable, a vessel unto dishonour.

"Doesn't the potter have authority over the clay to make of the same lump one vessel unto honour and another unto dishonour?" (Romans 9:21). The fallen mass of earthy Adam, mankind, is that lump. Shall the potter be subject to the clay? To think so is a poison to the soul.

In ancient households certain poison substances that could not be adequately washed away were stored only in vessels of dishonour, utility containers that were intended to be shattered and destroyed after they were used. But, the precious antidote against a poison was to be preserved carefully in a vessel intended to be honoured.

by- Edward E. Crawford

A BIOGRAPHICAL SKETCH
OF CHRISTOPHER NESS

Christopher Ness (1621-1705) was an English Nonconformist preacher and author.

He wrote *"A History and Mystery of the Old and New Testaments,"* a work to which Matthew Henry is thought to owe much of his most valuable material for his commentary; *"A Protestant Antidote Against the Poison of Popery;" "The Crown and Glory of a Christian;" "A Christian's Walk and Work on Earth;" "A Church History from Adam,"* and *"A Scripture Prophecy to the End of the World;" "A Discovery of the Person and Period of Antichrist;"* and *"An Antidote Against Arminianism,"* a small work embodying in a brief form the doctrines on election, predestination, etc., as taught by John Owen, Toplady, and others.

Ness was born on Dec. 22, 1621 at North Cave, in the East Riding of Yorkshire, the son of Thomas Ness, a husbandman there. He was educated at a private school at North Cave, under Lazarus Seaman, and entered St. John's College, Cambridge, on May 17, 1638, where he graduated B.A. and M.A. When 23 years old he retired into Yorkshire, where he became a preacher of independent tenets successively at Cliffe, or South Cliffe Chapel in his native parish, in Holderness, and at Beverley, where he taught a school. On Dr. Winter's election as provost of Trinity College, Dublin, in 1651, Ness was chosen as his successor in the living of Cottingham, near Hull, though it does not appear that he ever received Episcopal orders.

In 1656, he became a preacher at Leeds, and in 1660 he was a lecturer under the vicar, Dr. Lake, afterwards Bishop of Chichester; but his Calvinism clashed with the Arminianiasm of Dr. Lake, and on St. Bartholomew's day in 1662 he was ejected from his lectureship. After this he became a schoolmaster and private preacher at Clayton, Morley, and Hunslet, all in Yorkshire. At Hunslet he took an indulgence as a Congregationalist in 1672, and a new meeting-house was opened by him on June 3, 1672.

He was excommunicated no less than four times, and when in 1674 or 1675 a writ *de excommunicato capiendo* was issued against him, he removed to London, where he preached to a private congregation in Salisbury Court, Fleet Street. In 1684 he had to conceal himself from the officers of the crown, who had a warrant for his arrest on the charge of publishing an elegy on the death of his friend John Partridge, another nonconformist minister. He died on Dec. 26, 1705, aged exactly 84 years, and was buried at Bunhill Fields cemetery.

I

AUTHOR'S PREFACE

Candid Reader, observe these few considerations: although this small manual be very little in itself and substance, yet ought it not therefore to be despised; for

First. We read how the mighty angel of the Covenant had a very little book open in his hand, (Rev. 10:2), yet this little book contained the great concerns of the Redeemer's little, little flock; a double diminutive as Christ calls them in Luke 12:32. And that little book was not shut nor sealed, but it was open. It is the work of Antichrist to keep it shut. Yea, it must also be eaten; "take it and eat it up." (Rev. 10:9); that is, it must go down and be hid in our hearts ("Thy Word have I hid in mine heart," Psa. 110:11); then the simplest soul may have right conceptions of it. "The word [is then] very nigh unto thee, in thy mouth, and in thy heart, that thou mayest do it" (Deut. 30:14).

Secondly. This little book hath cost me great study and labor to compose it, that it might contain the very cream and quintessence of the best Authors on this subject. Moreover, it hath cost me likewise many ardent prayers to God, and many earnest wrestlings with God, that I might not be one "of those that rebel against the light" (Job 24:13); but that in His light I might see light, (Psa. 36:9); and to have mine eyes anointed with Christ's eye-salve, (Rev. 3:18), that I might see clearly into these profound points, which hath so very much puzzled the Christian world. As blessed Athanasius sighed out in his day, "The world is overrun with **Arianism**;" so it is the sad sigh of our present times, the Christian world is overrun, yea, overwhelmed with the flood of **Arminianism**; which cometh, as it were, out of the mouth of the serpent, that he might cause the woman [the Church] "to be carried away of the flood" thereof (Rev. 12:15).

Thirdly, Lest this overflowing deluge of Arminianism should bring destruction upon us, there is great need that some servants of Christ should run to stop the further spreading of this plague and leprosy. Thus Moses stood in the gap, and prevented the destruction of Israel (Psa. 105:23). Also (Num. 16:48), "He stood between the dead and the living; and the plague was stayed." And the neglect of this duty the Lord complains of, that He found none of His servants to stand in the gap, etc. "O Israel, thy prophets are like the foxes in the deserts. Ye have not gone up into the gaps, neither made up the hedge for the house of Israel to stand in the battle in the day of the Lord . . . . With lies

II

ye have made the heart of the righteous sad, whom I have not made sad; and strengthened the hands of the wicked, . . . by promising him life'' (Ezek. 13:4,5,22). While I was considering these things, the Lord stirred up my spirit to do as is done in common conflagrations, when every one runs with the best bucket he can get, wherewith to quench the devouring flames, and to stop them, that they may not lay waste all before them.

Fourthly, when I had completed this short compendium I showed it to Dr. John Owen, Mr. Nicholas Lockier, and Mr. George Griffith, who all unanimously approved of it and wrote an epistle commendatory to it, subscribing it with all their three hands, which is too large here to insert, but the truth of the premises I do hereby affirm.

Lastly, as a little map doth represent a large country at one view, which will take much time to travel over, so this book is **multum in parvo,**much in a little. Read it seriously without partiality, and the Lord give you understanding in all things.
So prayeth.   Yours in the best of bonds,
                                                      CHRISTOPHER NESS
September 30th, 1700.

AN ANTIDOTE AGAINST ARMINIANISM

Of Arminianism In General

It hath ever been the lot of truth (like the Lord of it) to be crucified between right-hand and left-hand thieves. Truth's enemies, on all hands, are various. While some men consider the Bible to be an imposition on the world, and treat salvation by Christ as mere priestcraft and deception, there are others who tell us they have Christ, and are one with Christ, and yet with audacious effrontery cry down the ordinances of the gospel, and consider the means of grace as too burdensome for a free-born conscience, and too low and carnal for a seraphic spirit. There is as much beyond the truth as on this side thereof; as much in outrunning the flock of Christ and the Lamb that leads them, as in straggling and loitering behind. Truth hath evermore observed the golden mean.

The Socinians decry the divinity of Christ and His satisfaction, as if His sufferings were **exemplary** only, not **expiatory**. The Roman Catholics turn the true worship of God into will worship, and teach their own traditions for the commandments of God, spoiling God's institutions with man's inventions. And the **Arminians** do call the justice of God to the bar of reason; they dare confidently wade in the deep ocean of divine mysteries, and in stating the decrees of

God, where blessed Paul could find no bottom, but cried out "O the depth"etc. (Rom. 11:33); they dare undertake to fetch the Apostle from off his nonplus, saying, "God foresaw that Jacob **would** believe, and that Esau **would not** believe; therefore, the one was loved and the other hated." Thus Arminius' school teacheth deeper divinity than what Paul learned in the third heaven. And they do not only with the Socinians, gratify the pride of man's reason, but also the pride of man's **will**, in extenuating and lessening both the guilt and filth of original sin; even as Popery, their elder sister, doth gratify the pride of outward sense.

Hence Dr. Leighton calls Arminianism "the Pope's Benjamin, the last and greatest monster of the man of sin; the elixir of Anti-Christianism; the mystery of the mystery of iniquity; the Pope's cabinet; the very quintessence of equivocation." Alike hereunto Mr. Rous (Master of Eton College) addeth, saying, "Arminianism is the spawn of Popery, which the warmth of favour may easily turn into frogs of the bottomless pit." And what are the new Arminians but the varnished offspring of the old Pelagians, that makes the grace of God to lacquey it at the foot, or rather, the will of man? that makes the sheep to keep the shepherd? that puts God into the same extremity with Darius, who would gladly have saved Daniel but could not (Dan. 6:14)?

What else can their doctrine signify which they call a prescience or foreknowledge in God, the truth whereof depends, not on the decree of God, but on the free-will of the creature? This is to make the creature have no dependence on the Creator, and to fetter Divine Providence. Thus that fatal necessity, which they would lay at our doors, unavoidably remains at theirs, and (according to their scheme) God must say thus to man, "O My poor creature! that fatal fortune which hath harmed you must be endured more than bewailed, for it was from all eternity, before My providence. I could not hinder, I could not but consent to those fatal contingencies; and unavoidable Fate hath, whether I will or no, pronounced the inevitable sentence." What else is this but to overthrow all those graces of Faith, Hope, etc., to expectorate (to cast off) all vital godliness; and to pull the great Jehovah Himself out of His throne of glory, setting up dame Fortune to be worshipped in His stead?

These and many other great abominations have been discovered in the "chambers of imagery" in our days, and are nothing but measuring supernatural mysteries with the crooked metewand of degenerate reason. "Wisdom is too high for a fool'' (Prov. 24:7). In these points it was once well said, "Give me a mortified reason," for, to prescribe to God's infinite understanding, and to allow Him no reasons to guide His determinations by, but what we are acquainted with, is extremely arrogant. Reason must neither be the rule to measure faith by, nor the judge thereof. We may give a reason of our believing, to wit, "because it is written," but not of all things believed, as why Jacob was loved and Esau hated before they had done either good or evil—this was the counsel of God's own will. Touching such sublime mysteries our faith stands upon two sure bottoms: the first is, that being, wisdom, and power of God doth infinitely transcend ours; so may reveal matters far above our reach; the second is; that whatsoever God reveals is undoubtedly true, and to be believed, although the bottom of it cannot be sounded by the line of our reason; because man's reason is not absolute, but variously limited, perplexed with his own frailty, and defective in its own acting.

CHAPTER I

OF PREDESTINATION

That the reader may have clear views of the doctrine of Predestination, I shall, first, state that doctrine as revealed in the Bible; second, consider the Arminian's view thereof, viz., that it is conditional upon the foresight of faith, works, perseverance, etc., and, thirdly, answer the objections brought by the Arminians against the Scriptural doctrine of Election and Predestination.

The Doctrine of Predestination

Predestination is the decree of God, whereby (according to the counsel of His own will) He fore-ordained some of mankind to eternal life, and refused or passed by others; for the praise of His glorious mercy and justice. Some are vessels of mercy, others are vessels of wrath. "Hath not the potter power over the clay, of the same lump to make one vessel unto honour, and another unto dishonour? What if God, willing to show His wrath, and to make His power known, endured with much long-suffering the vessels of wrath fitted to destruction; And that He might make known the riches of His glory on the vessels

5

of mercy, which He had afore prepared unto glory?'' (Rom. 9:21-23).

In a great house are various vessels both for use and ornament; vessels of honour, and vessels of dishonour, (2 Tim. 2:20); and the master of the house hath a right to, and can wisely use, all his vessels, even as he shall think proper. God hath His use even of Pharaoh and of the church's greatest enemies; if it be but scullion work, to brighten vessels of mercy by them. God hath appointed the Elect unto Glory; and He hath by the eternal and most free purpose of His will fore-ordained all the means thereunto; such as redemption by Christ, regeneration by the Holy Ghost, effectual calling and conversion, justification in the court of conscience by saving faith in Jesus' merits, sanctification in the heart by the Spirit, producing holy living and holy walking with God and man. And these blessed participators are ''kept by the power of God through faith unto salvation'' (I Pet. 1:5). ''Whom He did predestinate, them He also called: and whom He called, them He also justified: and whom He justified, them He also glorified. What shall we then say to these things?'' (Rom. 8:30,31). We will say with the apostle, ''God hath not appointed us to wrath, but to obtain salvation'' (I Thess. 5:9).

It is called destination, as it comprehends a determined order of the means to the end; and pre-destination, because God appointed this order in and with Himself before the actual existence of those things so ordered. The Greek word signifies a fore-separating for God's special use; as Israel was separated from among all the nations of the world to be God's peculiar inheritance. "I am the Lord your God, which have separated you from other people" (Lev. 20:24). "The Lord thy God hath chosen thee to be a special people unto Himself, above all people that are upon the face of the earth" (Deut. 7:6). I have separated you to become vessels of mercy, members of Christ, and temples of the Holy Ghost, before all time, even from all eternity. As Divine prescience is sometimes largely taken for predestation, "God hath not cast away His people which He foreknew" (Rom. 11:2), that is, whom He did predestinate; so, in like manner, predestation is taken strictly and in part for election itself (Rom. 8:30; Eph. 1:5). I shall handle it accordingly in this following treatise, using the words Election and Predestination promiscuously.

Predestination is also called a **Divine decree**, for in it is the determinate counsel of God, and the counsel of His own will, in bringing to pass such ends by such and such means. "For of a truth against Thy holy child Jesus . . . Herod . . . were gathered together, for to do whatsoever Thy hand and Thy counsel determined before to be.

done'' (Acts 4:27,28). "Having predestinated us
. . . . according to the good pleasure of His will"
(Eph. 1:5). "Being predestinated according to
the purpose of Him who worketh all things after
the counsel of His own will" (ver. 11). The election and predestination of the Lord is, in Scripture phrase, termed the "hand," the "determinate counsel," the "purpose," the "good
pleasure" of God (Acts 2:23; Eph. 1:9).

The Divine decree of Predestination hath
various properties; it is eternal, unchangeable,
absolute, free, discriminating, and extensive.

The First Property of the Divine Decree; it is
ETERNAL

This is proved from the following reasons:

1. God's internal and immanent acts are the
same with His essence: such an act is the Divine
decree; and, therefore, as God's essence is eternal, so His decree must be eternal also. Now the
decree is God's decreeing, because whatever is in
God is God; it is God Himself by one eternal act,
decreeing and determining whatsoever should
come to pass unto the praise of His own glory.

2. The second reason is deduced from the
simplicity of God, which is, God considered as
one mere and perfect act, without any composi-

8

tion or succession. There can be no more a new thought, a new intent, or a new purpose in God, than there can be a new God. Whatever God thinks He ever thought, and always doth and will think. Whatever God purposes He always purposed, and ever and doth and will purpose. He saith, "I know the thoughts I think toward you, saith the Lord, thoughts of peace, and not of evil, to give you an expected end" (Jer. 29:11). As He cannot know anything new, neither can He intend anything new, for His name is, I AM. He takes not new counsels, as man, neither draws up new determinations.

3. The third reason is taken from Christ. If Christ was the Lamb slain from the foundation of the world (as He is called, Rev. 13:8), then predestination to life must needs be before time, because Christ is the Foundation of election. We are elected in Him. "According as He hath chosen us in Him before the foundation of the world" (Eph. 1:4); and predestinated by Him, "Having predestinated us unto the adoption of children by Jesus Christ to Himself" (Eph. 1:5). Christ is the means. Now the end cannot be of a later date and determination than the means to that end; they have relations to each other. And if Christ be the eternal purpose of the Father, the act of electing in Christ must needs be His eternal purpose also.

4. Scripture expressly proves the **eternity** of the decree, saying, it was "before the world began" (II Tim. 1:9; Titus 1:2); and "before the foundation of the world" (Eph. 1:4); and it was an "eternal purpose which He purposed in Christ Jesus our Lord" (Eph. 3:11).

5. It is the royal prerogative of the great Jehovah to order as well as appoint things that are coming and that shall come: "I appointed the ancient people, and the things that are coming and shall come" (Isa. 44:7). None can appoint God the time. He saith, "Who is like Me? and who will appoint Me the time?" (Jer. 50:44). Hence time is said to travail with those eternal decrees of God, and brings forth the accomplishment of them in their proper season; and the decree will bring forth ("Before the decree bring forth," Zeph. 2:2). Every thing hath its accomplishment in time, which was decreed to fall out from all eternity.

6. If human concerns have this encomium that "these are ancient things" (I Chron. 4:22), how much more the Divine decree, which is not the work of yesterday! If the **negative** part of predestination (the ungodly) were "of old ordained" (Jude 4), then much more the **positive**, God's purpose of loving Jacob, as well as hating Esau, was before they had done "either good or evil" (Rom. 9:11).

Objection. Some may object, saying, We grant God's prescience or foreknowledge to be eternal, but not His predestination; that choice or election mentioned in I Cor. 1:27-29 must be a temporal, not an eternal, election.

Answers. I. With God, the knowledge of things that shall come to pass must follow the decree thereof; for things must first be decreed, and then foreseen in that being which they have in the decree; in this sense prescience presupposes predestination. "Known unto God are all His works from the beginning of the world" (Acts 15:18). God hath not an imperfect but a thorough foreknowledge of all future things; the means and the end; not only as they may be, but also as they shall be, by His Divine determination.

2. Prescience, or fore-knowledge, is taken for God's love from eternity. "Whom He did foreknow He also did predestinate" (Rom. 8:29); that is, "whom He fore-loved" so Zanchius reads it. Whom He foreknew, not only with the knowledge of observation, but with the knowledge of approbation also; He foreknew them to be His. So it is predestination itself; and to grant an eternal prescience without an eternal predestination, is to break the links of that golden chain in Rom. 8:29, 30. "God hath not," and God will not, "cast away His people which He foreknew" (Rom. 11:2).

11

3. Some grant a predestination eternal to the elect only, but to the non-elect only a prescience or naked foresight (without any pre-ordination), lest they should make God the author of the creature's sin and ruin. But these men fear where no fear is; for the worst evil that ever was committed in the world, to wit, the crucifying of the Prince of glory, Jesus Christ, did not only fall under the foreknowledge of God, but also under His determinate counsel, "Him being delivered by the determinate counsel and foreknowledge of God, ye have taken, and by wicked hands have crucified and slain" (Acts 2:23; 4:28); the taking and apprehension of Christ was not barely foreknown but unchangeably determined.

4. Even suppose it be granted that the apostle speaks of a temporal election, or choice, in I Cor. 1:27, etc., yet that signifies no more than our vocation or calling; and temporal reprobation intimates no more than man's obduration. The accomplishment of both these is granted to be in time, so may not be confounded with this eternal decree of God; these are but fruits and effects of that eternal decree.

Inferences drawn from the foregoing.

1. Is God's love eternal? Then Satan cannot get beyond or between this love of God and us; for it was before the world was, and so before Satan was.

2. Augustine told a curious fool that asked what God did before the world was made, "that He made hell for such as him;" but this teaches us that God was choosing us to Himself before the world began. O wonderful!

3. If so, believer, then thy saintship and sufferings have eternal glory wrapped up in them. All this comfort is lost in the contrary doctrine.

The Second Property of the Divine Decree of Predestination: it is UNCHANGEABLE.

Hence it is compared to "mountains of brass" (Zech. 6:1), and it is called, "immutability of His counsel" (Heb. 6:17). This is made evident by sundry reasons, as

I. The Divine decree hath an unchangeable fountain, to wit, the unchangeableness of God. "He is in one mind, and who can turn Him?" (Job 23:13). He desires and He doth it; no created being can interpose between the desire and the doing, to hinder their meeting together. "God is not a man, that He should lie; neither the son of man that He should repent" (Num. 23:19). "I am the Lord, I change not" (Mal. 3:6); with Him is no "variableness, neither shadow of turning" (Jas. 1:17). "The counsel of the Lord standeth for ever, the thoughts of His heart to all generations'' (Psa. 33:11). ''There are many devices in a man's heart; nevertheless the counsel of the Lord, that shall stand'' (Prov. 19:21). Man is a poor changeable creature and changes his mind oftener than his garment, both from the darkness of his understanding and the perverseness of his will; he frequently sees something that he saw not before; but there is no such imperfection in God, all things are naked before Him, dissected, or with their faces upward. ''Neither is there any creature that is not manifest in His sight; but all things are naked and opened unto the eyes of Him with whom we have to do'' (Heb. 4:13). He knows all His works (their natures and circumstances) as perfectly in the beginning of the world as He will do at the end thereof. And He abides still in one mind when His dispensations are changed, for He decreed the change of them from all eternity.

2. The decree of Election stands upon an unchangeable foundation, to wit, that Rock of ages, ''Jesus Christ, the same yesterday, and today, and forever'' (Heb. 13:8). As the first Adam was the foundation stone in the decree of creation, so the last Adam, even Jesus, is the foundation stone in the decree of election. God hath blessed us in Him, yea, and we shall be blessed; He hath chosen us in Him; pardoned us in Him; sealed us in Him; built us up and completed us in Him; ''According to His own pur-

pose and grace, which was given us in Christ Jesus before the world began'' (II Tim. 1:9); All those acts of grace are said to be in Christ, who hath blest us in Christ (Eph. 1:3); chosen us in Him (v. 4); pardoned us; "in whom we have redemption through His blood, the forgiveness of sins" (v. 7); "in whom also after that ye believed, ye were sealed" (v. 13); "rooted and built up in Him" (Col. 2:7): and ye are "complete in Him" (v. 10).

Indeed, Christ Himself was under Divine ordination; He "verily was fore-ordained before the foundation of the world" (I Pet. 1:20), and is called the elect stone (I Pet. 2:6). Christ is the first person elected. "Behold My servant whom I uphold, Mine elect" (Isa. 42:1; Matt. 12:18). Christ was chosen as the Head, and we as His members; therefore are we said to be given to Christ. "Thine they were, and Thou gavest them Me" (John 17:6). Now, so long as this foundation standeth sure, so long doth the superstructure remain unchangeable. The temple stood firmly upon those two pillars, Jachin and Boza, i. e., stability and strength; so the decree of election standeth sure upon Christ the Foundation; and none can pluck an elect soul from off this Foundation. None can pluck any of Christ's out of His hands. Christ will lose none that are given to him; He will fulfill His Father's will by taking care of them all. "And this is the Father's will which hath sent Me, that of all which He hath given Me I should lose nothing, but should raise it up again at the last day'' (John 6:39). ''They shall never perish'' (John 10:28).

3. 'Tis unchangeable, because it is a decree written in heaven, and so above the reach of either angry men or enraged devils to cancel. ''The Lord knoweth them that are His'' (2 Tim. 2:19), they are ''the general assembly and church of the first-born, which are written in heaven'' (Heb. 12:23). Thence it is called ''the Lamb's book of life,'' which contains a catalog of the elect, determined by the unalterable counsel of God; which number can neither be increased nor diminished. This is to be rejoiced in above dominion over devils; ''rather rejoice, because your names are in heaven'' (Luke 10:20); which, if our names may be written in heaven to-day and blotted out to-morrow would be no such ground of joy. If the decrees of the Medes and Persians, which were but earthly writings, were unalterable (Dan. 6:8), how much more the decrees of the great God, written in heaven, must be unchangeable. Must Pilate say, ''What I have written I have written'' (John 19:22); that is to say, ''my writing shall not be altered,'' and shall not God say so much more? ''I know (saith Solomon) that, whatsoever God doeth, it shall be for ever; nothing can be put to it, nor any thing taken from it'' (Ecc. 3:14). ''My counsel

shall stand, and I will do all My pleasure . . . I have spoken it, I will also bring it to pass; I have purposed it, I will also do it'' (Isa. 46:10,11). The sun may sooner be stopped in his course than God hindered of His work or in His will. Nature, angels, devils, men, may all be resisted, and so miss of their design; not so God: for ''who hath resisted His will?'' All those chariots of human occurences and dispensations come forth from between those mountains of brass, the unalterable decrees of God. (Zech. 6:1); and should it be granted that **one** soul may be blotted out of this book of life (this writing in heaven) then it is possible that **all** may be so; and, by consequence, it may be supposed that that book may become empty, and useless as waste paper; and that Christ may be a head without a body.

4. 'Tis unchangeable, for the decree concerning the end includes the means to that end, and binds them altogether with an irrefragable chain, which can never be broken. The predestinated, called, justified, glorified ones, are the same (Rom. 8:30). Therefore the purpose of God according to election must stand (Rom. 9:11). God doth not decree the end without the means, nor the means without the end, but both together. As a purpose for building includes the hewing of stone, and squaring of timber, and all other materials for building-work; and as a

17

decree for war implies arms, horses, ammunition, and all warlike provisions; so here, all that are elected to salvation, are elected to sanctification also. God ordains to the means as well as to the end. "As many as were ordained to eternal life believed" (Acts 13:48). God hath ordained that we should walk in good works (Eph. 2:10). We are elected unto obedience, through the "santification of the Spirit" (I Pet. 1:2); therefore God hath promised to sanctify those whom He purposed to save. We teach with Augustine that, "Election is an ordaining to grace as well as to glory." In pre-destination, therefore, the means of salvation are no less absolutely decreed than salvation itself. We may not conceive that God's decree runs after this form, "I will predestinate Peter to salvation, if it should so happen that he doth believe and persevere;" but rather thus, " I do predestinate Peter to salvation, which, that he may infallibly obtain, I will **give** him both faith and perseverance." Were it otherwise, the foundation would not stand sure; yea, and God's gifts would not be without repentance, if God did not absolutely decree to give and bestow faith and perseverance to His elected ones. The covenant of grace runs in this tenure, "I will be a God to you, and ye shall be a people unto Me" that is, I will make ye so.

Inferences drawn from the foregoing.

1. A name written in heaven, where no thief, no rust, no moth comes to destroy it, is better than to be enrolled in princely courts; 'tis a name better than of sons and daughters, to be a free citizen of heaven.

2. Though we are changeable creatures, yet unchangeable love is towards us, that keeps faster hold of us than we of it.

3. It is infinite condencension that the great God should hold a poor lump of clay so fast in His Almighty hands, as to secure our interest to all eternity (John 10:28, 29; I Pet. 1:4, 5).

The Third Property of the Divine Decree: it is ABSOLUTE

It is absolute in respect of the efficient impulsive cause which cannot be anything out of God, as the following reasons evince.

1. If the Divine decree be eternal it must be absolute; for nothing can be assigned before an eternal act, as the efficient cause thereof. There cannot be a cause of the will of God out of God. Predestination is an immanent act of the Divine will; and so, not only the cause, but also the first cause of all created beings; and therefore cannot (in any good sense) be said to depend on fore-

seen transient acts in the creature; so, by consequence, must be an absolute act, unless we will make the volitions of God to come behind the created and temporary volitions of man, which is grossly absurd. This goes to a denial of God being the first cause of all things.

2. First, if God be God; if He be an almighty, all wise, all free, and an all-disposing God, then His decree of Election must be absolute; for a conditional decree makes a conditional God, and plainly **ungods** Him, by ascribing such imperfections to Him as are unworthy His majesty, and below His Divine being; as, first, it opposes His omnipotence—if some conditions be antecedent to the will of God, then the same are antecedent also to the power of God. Second, it takes away the glory of the Divine wisdom in ordering all things; for if Peter must be willing to believe before God's decree concerning Peter, then Divine wisdom doth not determine concerning the order of things. Thirdly, it takes away the glory of God's absolute liberty and independence; for if Peter's believing and Judas's not believing be antecedent to the decree of God concerning them, then Peter and Judas make themselves the objects of election and non-election, and God hath not an absolute dominion over His own creatures; the potter hath not freedom to make this lump of clay a vessel of honour and that a vessel of dishonour, and the

difference will arise more from the quality of the clay than the will of the potter, and God's will must be dependent on the will of man for its determinations. This plainly overthrows the independency of God. Fourth, it takes away the glory of His all-disposing providence; if the decree be not absolute, how can God be said wholly to dispose of lots that are cast into the lap, as in Prov. 16:33? Shall we say that the lot of the apostleship fell to Matthias by chance (Act 1:26); was it not rather absolutely ordained and ordered by the Lord, to whom the Apostles prayed, as in v. 24, saying, "Thou, Lord, which knowest the hearts of all men, show whether (or which) of these two **Thou** has chosen . . . And they gave forth their lots; and the lot fell upon Matthias" (Acts 1:24, 26)? Thus by the disposal of lots in the lap was Achan discovered to be Israel's curse, and Saul appointed to be Israel's king (Jos. 7:14-18; I Sam. 10:19-21). Man purposeth, but God disposeth; because God by an absolute decree hath foreordained all things that do come to pass. They fall not out casually and beyond God's intention; thus it is said, "It behoved Christ to suffer" (Luke 24:46).

3. If the will of the potter be an absolute will over his pots, much more is the will of God an absolute will over mankind. It is God's own comparison (Rom. 9:20, 21). God compares not

Himself to a goldsmith, because a goldsmith hath costly materials, such as silver and gold, which lays some obligation on him to make honourable vessels therewith. But He compareth Himself to a potter, because first, the materials of a potter are vile and sordid, to wit, clay, so more answerable to fallen mankind, out of which God maketh His choice. We are not only clay (Job 4:19), but sinful clay through the fall. Second, the potter doth not make this difference among his pots for any foreseen inherent goodness in his clay (for the whole lump before him is of an equal temper and quality), but from the pleasure of his own will. Thus the potter's power over his materials is clearer from exception than that of the goldsmith, and illustrates more the absoluteness of God's will in His choice both in vessels of honour and vessels of dishonour. Again, the distance between the clay and potter is but a finite distance, even the distance only between one creature and another, animate and inanimate; but the distance between God and mankind is infinite, not only the natural distance between God and us, as we are creatures, but also the moral distance between us, as we are sinners. The potter also must have his clay made to his hand; he cannot make his own clay, though he may temper it for his work when he hath found it; but the great God creates His own clay. He created the earth out of which man was formed. "In the beginning God created the heaven and the earth" (Gen. 1:1). "And the Lord God formed man of the dust of the ground" (Gen. 2:7). It follows then, if the potter by an absolute will disposes of his pots, much more hath God a right concerning His creatures.

Inferences drawn from the preceding.

1. If the absolute will of God be the universal cause of all things, then no event can fall beyond or beside God's will; and fortune (in the world's sense thereof) is but the devil's blasphemous spit upon Divine providence.

2. God's absolute will cannot be resisted; as He hath willed, so shall it come to pass; and there is no hindering the execution thereof. "The Lord of hosts hath sworn, saying, Surely as I have thought, so shall it come to pass; and as I have purposed, so shall it stand" (Isa. 14:24). "Our God is in the heavens: He hath done whatsoever He hath pleased" (Psa. 115:3) "I know that Thou canst do everything" (Job 42:2).

3. Then let us learn submission to the will of God. Proud, yet brittle clay, will be knocking their sides against the absolute will of God, till they break in pieces; so did Adonijah, when Solomon must rule; compare I Kings 1:5 with I Chron. 22:9, and mark the end thereof, I Kings

2:23-25. O for the grace of humility to enable us to adopt the language of the prophet, ''Now, O Lord, Thou art our Father; we are the clay, and Thou our Potter, and we all are the work of Thy hand'' (Isa. 64:8).

The Fourth Property of the Divine Decree: it is FREE

As the Divine decree is not conditional but absolute, so 'tis not of necessity but free, as flowing only from the pleasure of God's will. God is a free agent, and cannot fall under any obligation, so as to necessitate Him in any of His emanations to the creature; but He is graciously pleased of His own free love to oblige Himself.

1. The first argument to prove the freeness of the Divine decree is—such a decree as passeth without any obligation to necessitate the passing thereof, must needs have the property of freeness; and thus it was with the Divine decree. If there be any obligation it must be either in respect of objects or acts or motives; but God was not obliged in any of these respects.

First. He was not obliged in respect of objects, for God was under no necessity of having either any elect or any reprobate. He was happy in Himself from all eternity; would have been happy for ever without either of these; and to affirm that God stood in need of any such objects is to

24

deny the perfections of God. If it is called humbling Himself to look down on things in heaven, much more on things on earth.

Second. He was not obliged by acts, as acts are necessary by a moral obligation. God was under no moral obligation to man. He had done man no wrong if He had never willed man to be, much less to be holy and happy. God was not bound to any of His actions concerning man; He cannot be a debtor to many any other way than as He makes Himself a debtor of His own good pleasure. As in His promises His love moved Him to make them, and His truth binds Him to perform them, otherwise those actions would be actions of debt, and not acts of grace, contrary to the tenor of Scripture, which makes the whole work of man's salvation to flow wholly from the free grace of God.

Third. He was not obliged in respect to motives; neither in the creature, nor yet in Christ. Not in the creature, for the being of the creature (much more the faith and good works of the creature) was the effect of the decree of God, so could not be the motive thereof. Nor could the Lord foresee repentance, faith, love etc., in the creature, antecedent to His own purpose in the gift thereof. Neither is Christ Himself the moving cause of the Divine decree; for Christ is the effect of God's eternal love, not the cause thereof. "God so loved the world that He gave

His Son'' (John 3:16). God's love gives Christ. Therefore we are said to be elected in Christ, but never for Christ; for Christ is an elect one Himself, as was shown before. Christ was first chosen, then the members. The love of God as immediately cometh from Himself to me, as to Christ; and He was foreordained to be our Head, and we to be His members. Thus we are Christ's; and Christ is God's as the effect of His love to His elect from all eternity (I Cor. 3:22).

2. The second argument to prove the freeness of Divine decree is taken from the testimony of the Word of God (the Bible) in which it is affirmed to be a free act, an act of grace and not of debt, an act of love and special favour, founded upon the mere good pleasure of God. "Even so, Father: for so it seemed good in Thy sight" (Matt. 11:26). "It is your Father's good pleasure to give you the kingdom" (Luke 12:32). It was a gracious purpose in God from all eternity (2 Tim. 1:9; Eph. 1:5, 9, 11). Paul's repeated exclamation is, "the pleasure of His own will," "the counsel of His own will;" but more fully in Rom. 9:13, 16 doth he exemplify this truth in Jacob and Esau. "Jacob have I loved, but Esau have I hated . . . It is not of him that willeth, nor of him that runneth, but of God that sheweth mercy." Both Malachi the Prophet (Mal. 1:3), and Paul the Apostle make this instance of Jacob and Esau the fullest exemplification of free elec-

tion. For they lay together in the same womb, and were born at the same time (for Jacob took hold of Esau's heel), so the contrary disposal of these two doth more illustrate the free predestination of God than any other two whatsoever. Of Jacob there came a distinguished people from all the world, even a Church unto God; and of Esau there sprang forth a persecuting seed. God hath no regard to faith in the one, or of infidelity in the other. When God's oracle passed upon them, they were both in their mother's womb, conceived in sin; and, if there were any pre-eminence, Esau had it, as being the first-born. What then cast the balance? Nothing but the good pleasure of God. God will "have mercy on whom He will have mercy, and whom He will He hardeneth" (Rom. 9:18). Now, in opposition to this carnal reason saith, "It was because God foresaw what they would be." Nay, but God loved them because He loved them (Deut. 7:7, 8). It was choosing love that He bare to them, and that is the best of the kind. That is the favour which God bears to His people: He loved them, and chose them for His own.

3. The third reason to prove the freeness of the Divine decree is: God hath in all ages given us examples of His free receiving some of mankind and rejecting others; this is plain from Scripture history. Of Adam's three sons, Cain, Abel, Seth, the eldest was rejected. Of Noah's three,

Japheth, Shem and Ham, the youngest was rejected. Of Terah's three, Abraham, Nahor, Haran, the middlemost was rejected; for Nahor was an idolator, and Laban sware by Nahor's idol (compare Gen. 31:53 with Jos. 24:2). Now why this picking and choosing, this receiving and rejecting; eldest at one time, youngest at another time, and middlemost at a third time? What is all this but to show that neither birth nor age, nor anything foreseen or existing in the creature, can produce any claim, but that all lies in the free election of God! We can give no reason, save the good pleasure of God, why Pharaoh and Nebuchadnezzar (both engaged in the same warfare against Israel, the church of God) had different dispensations of heaven upon them; the one was hardened and the other humbled; why Pharaoh's Baker was hanged and his butler restored to his office again; why two men shall be in one bed, the one taken, the other left; why two women shall be grinding at one mill, the one taken, the other left; why Aaron's rod, of all twelve, only blossomed.

4. If the fruits of the Divine decree be free, then must the decree itself be free. This assumption is clear, for first, our vocation is from free love. Christ freely, and of His own sovereign will, called James and John, the two sons of Zebedee, and left their father uncalled with the hired servants (Mark 1:20). ''He called unto Him

whom He would" (Mark 3:13). "It is given unto you to know the mysteries of the kingdom of heaven, but to them it is not given" (Matt. 13:11). "We know that the Son of God is come, and hath given us an understanding, that we may know Him that is true" (I John 5:20). "Thou hast hid these things from the wise and prudent, and hast revealed them unto babes. Even so, Father: for so it seemed good in Thy sight" (Matt. 11:26). Second, our sanctification is from free grace. Of His own will He begat us (Jas. 1:18). The sanctifying grace breathes where it listeth; and the wind at sea, is as much at our command as the fresh gales of this renewing Spirit. Third, our glorification is free. Eternal life is the gift of God (Rom. 6:23); He doth not sell it for foreseen faith or works, but He freely gives it. Now if all these fruits of election be free, then the election itself to these fruits must be free also. If faith be the free gift of God (Eph. 2:8), then predestination to faith must of necessity be also free, for God worketh all things according to the counsel of His own will (Eph. 1:11).

Christian believer, there is much comfort and establishment to be drawn from a view of the freeness of the grace of God; then

1. Admire free grace in this decree of predestination, and cry, How is it, Lord, that Thou dost manifest Thyself and Thy love to me, and not unto the world (John 14:22)?

2. Thou makest not thyself to differ from others, but free grace does it for thee. Thou art a lump of clay in the hands of the potter, no better than others; yea, pressed down to hell by Adam's fall; that God should lift thee up to heaven, be thankful.

3. Rejoice in the Lord, sing to the honour of His great name, and live to His praise and glory. Did David dance before the Lord with all his might? Did he say to Michal, "It was before the Lord, who chose me before they father, to appoint me ruler over . . . Israel; therefore will I play before the Lord" (2 Sam. 6:14, 21)? David's appointment, at that time, was but to an earthly kingdom; thou art freely chosen to inherit an heavenly: therefore I say rejoice.

The Fifth Property of the Divine Decree: It Is DISCRIMINATING

That it is discriminating and particular, not universal or general, may be proved from the following arguments:

1. The very word used, **Election,** confutes the universality of it. There can be no choice made, where all are taken, and none left. That cannot be called election which is equally extended to every individual. He doth not elect that doth not prefer some before others. God did not choose

all the thirty-two thousand Israelites that were with Gideon, to save Israel by, out of the hand of Midian, but only the three hundred that lapped; and these were chosen from out of the thirty and two thousand (Judges 7:3-7). God did not choose all the nations, but only Israel, to be a special people to Himself, "Thy God hath chosen thee . . . above all people that are upon the face of the earth" (Deut. 7:6). Election **must** therefore be discriminating, and a making of some to differ from others.

2. Scripture expressly states that only few are chosen, though many be called (Matt. 20:16). It is only a little flock (Luke 12:32), and but one of a city and two of a family that are brought to Zion (Jer. 3:14). "I have chosen you out of the world," saith Christ (John 15:19); and the Lord calls Paul a chosen vessel unto Him (Act 9:15; 22:14). How ill it sounds in the ears of a gospel-spirit to say that Pharaoh and Judas were elected as well as Paul and Barnabas; and that Simon Magus was elected as well as Simon Peter; all which a general election, which is the Arminian hypothesis, most necessarily asserteth. How can these "reprobate silver" pieces be, in a gospel sense, termed chosen vessels (as Paul was) to know God's will, and see the Just One (Acts 22:14)?

3. If election be general under a condition of believing, then Pilate, Caiphas, and Judas were

elected under that condition; and so God is brought in to speak after this manner: I have appointed to save Pilate, Caiphas and Judas if they will believe in the death of Christ; but, if they believe, Christ shall not be crucified, for those are the very men appointed by My determinate counsel to put Christ to death (see Acts 2:23; 4:28). Had these men believed (and they have believed according to the Arminians' views), then God's decree concerning Christ's death would not have been absolute, but depending on a condition which those men might have fulfilled (to wit, believing in Christ's death), which had they done, they had believed in that which then never would have come to pass. Thus carnal reason bespatters Divine wisdom!

4. How can it be safely said that God ever intended the salvation of any others, but those who are, of shall be, effectually saved? This would frustrate the will of God, even His will of intention, and would be contrary to the following scriptures, **"Our God . . . hath done whatsoever He hath pleased"** (Psa. 115:3). "I know that Thou canst do every thing, and that no thought can be withholden from Thee" (Job 42:2). And no man can resist the will of God, for He will have mercy on whom He will have mercy, and whom He will He hardeneth. And, if after all, O vain man! thou wilt still object, and say, "Why doth He yet find fault? for who hath

resisted His will?'' the only answer for thee is, "Nay but, O man, who art thou that repliest against God? Shall the thing formed say to Him that formed it, Why hast thou made me thus?'' (Rom. 9:19). Thus it was, **according to the sovereign will of Jehovah,** that Jacob and Esau were discriminated the one from the other.

5. The apostle showeth that there is this discriminating difference between man and man, that some are chosen to life, and therefore shall most certainly obtain it! others are refused and left in a perishing condition, which they shall as certainly not escape. "The election hath obtained it, and the rest were blinded'' (Rom. 11:7). The difference is of God, according to the purpose of election; not as of Him that foresees faith or works, but as of Him that gives both.

We may learn from the preceding:

1. It is distinguishing love that our Potter hath made us what we are, men and women. All creatures, even toads and other obnoxious animals, were formed of the same dust with man. "The Lord God formed man of the dust of the ground'' (Gen. 2:7); "and out of the ground the Lord God formed every beast'' (Gen. 1:19).

2. It is the will of God that some be poor and others rich; so here, that some be vessels of honor, and others of dishonor.

3. Christ raised not all up that were dead, but Lazarus, etc., nor all that were born blind, but

him mentioned in John 9. Bless God for raising thee up from thy death of sin, and healing thy blindness, and not others! Thou wert alike undeserving with them! Thou wert, thou art still, in thyself, a sinner! And if thou art taught by grace, the last accents on thy faltering tongue will be the publican's prayer. "God be merciful to me a sinner."

The Sixth and last Property of the Divine Decree; it is
EXTENSIVE

The Divine decree of God's electing and predestinating love, although discriminating and particular, is, nevertheless, very extensive. "I beheld, and lo, a great multitude, which no man could number, of all nations, and kindreds, and people, and tongues, stood before the throne, and before the Lamb . . . and cried with a loud voice, saying Salvation" (Rev. 7:9). There is a general decree that relates to all created beings, both animate and inanimate, celestial and terrestial; and extends itself to every individual in the whole creation of God. For as it gave a being to all things, so it preserves them in that being while they continue in the world; and the work of Providence, which extends itself from angels to worms, succeeds the work of creation.

Now although this special Divine decree of predestination extends not (as the general decree) to every individual, it is nevertheless very extensive, even to all ranks, sexes, ages, nations and generations.

1. To all **ranks**. To all sorts and ranks of men, to princes and peasants, to high and low, to rich and poor, to bond and free. It extends itself to kings, for among them hath God His chosen vessels—His Davids, His Solomons, His Hezekiahs, His Mannassehs. Though the Scriptures say (I Cor. 1:26) "Not many mighty, not many noble, are called," yet it doth not say, not any; for God hath had some great ones to own His ways in all ages. It extends to servants also (Titus 2:9, 11), for God bestows His love on those in rags as well as those in robes. The poor have the gospel preached unto them (Matt. 11:5), and God is no respector of persons.

2. To all **sexes**. To both sexes is the decree extended, to male and female. God hath His elect ladies. "The elder unto the elect lady and her children, whom I love in the truth;" and "The children of thy elect sister, greet thee" (2 John 1:13), and both male and female are one in Christ Jesus (Gal. 3:28) "I entreat thee also, true yoke-fellow, help those women, which laboured with me in the gospel . . . whose names are in the book of life" (Phil. 4:3).

3. To all **ages.** To young and old, to children, and to those of riper years; yea, very infants lay in the womb of the eteranl decree, before ever they came out of their mother's womb. "Before I formed thee in the belly I knew thee; and before thou camest forth out of the womb I sanctified thee; and I ordained thee a prophet unto the nations" (Jer. 1:5). John Baptist was filled with the Holy Ghost, even from the womb (Luke 1:15); and it is probable David believed that his child belonged to the election of grace, and that its soul was bound up in the bundle of life; for he comforted himself thus; "I shall go to him, but he shall not return to me" (2 Sam. 12:23). David's going to the grave to it could yield him but little comfort.

4. To all **nations.** Grace is not immured within the walls of one nation only, but is extended to Jew and Gentile, to circumcision and uncircumcision, to Barbarian and Scythian, bond and free (Col. 3:11), to some of every nation under heaven (Acts 2:5). The partition wall, which was betwixt Jew and Gentile, is thrown down. Our Lord saith, "and other sheep I have which are not of this (the Jewish) fold: them also I must bring" (John 10:16). This predestinating love effectually calls its chosen ones from all quarters. "I have loved thee; therefore, I will bring thy seed from the east, and gather thee from the west; I will say to the north, Give up: and to the

south, Keep not back; bring My sons from afar, and My daughters from the ends of the earth; Even every one that is called by My name" (Isa. 43:4-7).

5. To all **generations**. Predestinating love is like a river that runs under ground, and breaks out in certain places above the earth. To this river, this ocean of everlasting love, Moses had his eye, when of Joseph he said, "Blessed of the Lord be his land . . . for the deep that coucheth beneath" (Deut. 33:13). So fresh veins of election breaketh forth, sometimes in one generation, and sometimes in another. It is not bound up as to time—neither before the law, nor under the law, nor after the law; but, in every generation God hath His Church visible on the earth, and the gates of hell cannot prevail against it. As God is no respecter of persons, so neither is He of places, nations, or generations; but hath had, and He will have, His hidden ones to the world's end.

O believer! there is ground for much rejoicing, and strong consolation, in a view of the extensiveness of God's everlasting love.

1. If predestinating love extends itself to all degrees, then, they which are poor of wealth may be rich in faith, and a master's servant may be the Lord's freeman.

2. If to both sexes, then the weaker vessel may be a chosen vessel, and an heir of the grace of life.

3. If to all ages, then believing parents may have hope of their dying children; they may belong to the election of grace; they may be bound up in the swaddling bands of the covenant of grace; so they are not as without hope for them.

4. If to all nations, then the ends of the earth may look towards Christ (as He is lifted up on the pole of the everlasting Gospel) and be saved (Isa. 45:22).

5. If to all generations, then predestinating love is an inexhaustible fountain! crying always, Is there yet any of the house of the Lord among mankind that I may shew the kindness of God unto (2 Sam. 9:3)?

Of Conditional Predestination

Having stated the doctrine of Divine predestination, as revealed in the Scriptures, and having, from the same source, proved that it is possessed of various distinguishing properties, such as eternal, unchangeable, absolute, free, discriminating, and extensive; I come now, secondly, to consider the **Arminians'** view thereof, viz.: "That it is conditional, upon the foresight of faith, works, perseverance," etc.

To this I answer, that predestination cannot be conditional, upon a foresight of man's faith, works, or perseverance, etc., because of the twelve following reasons:—

1. That which the Scriptures declare to be the cause and ground of our election, that, and that only, must be the cause and ground thereof.

The good pleasure of God is the only cause and ground of our election, not any foresight of our faith, etc. That the Scriptures declare this, appears plain from Eph. 1:5; "According to the good pleasure of His will," and from Eph. 1:9 "Having made known to us the mystery of His will, according to His good pleasure;" and, "predestinated according to the purpose of Him who worketh all things after the counsel of His own will". Also, from Matt. 11:25, 26: "Thou hast hid these things from the wise and prudent, and hast revealed them unto babes." But why so? It is "Even so, Father: for so it seemed good in Thy sight." Again the Scriptures fully declare the same truth in Rom. 9:11-15, and 11:5; and in 2 Tim. 1:9, our salvation and vocation is stated to be, "not according to our works, but according to His own purpose and grace, which was given us in Christ Jesus before the world began." The time would fail me in enumerating more passages of Scripture, for the whole Bible as with one voice crieth aloud, election is of sovereign grace and not of works; flowing only from the absolute will and good pleasure of God.

2. That which makes election an action of debt ought not to be received; and the conditional decree doth this.

An action of grace, and an action of debt, are contradictory terms. If election be an act of grace (and the whole work of salvation hath been proved to be wholly and solely from free grace, p.17), then 'tis abominable and to be rejected to make it an act of debt. If the decree be conditional (upon foreseen faith and perseverance), then is it an act of debt and not of grace, an act of justice and not of mercy; for a decree of giving glory to believers persevering, as their reward, can be nothing else but remunerative justice.

3. That which makes God go out of Himself, in His immanent and eternal actings, ought not to be received; and the conditional decree doth so.

It makes God look upon this or that in the creature upon which the will of God is determined; thus man is the author of his own salvation, and God is not the author thereof. The doctrine of the conditional decree sets God upon His watch-tower of foreknowledge to espy what men will do; whether they will believe or no, obey or no, persevere or no, and according to His observation of their actings, so He determines His will concerning them; thus the perfection both of the

Divine knowledge and Divine will is with one breath denied.

4. No temporal thing can be the efficient cause of our eternal election; but faith, obedience, etc., are temporal things, the former being wrought in us, and the latter performed by us, in their appointed time.

What is this but to prefer time before eternity, and to set up a post- destination instead of a predestination?

5. That which is the fruit and effect of the Divine decree cannot be the cause thereof; and faith, preseverance, etc., are but the fruits and effects of electing love.

Such as are given to Christ in the decree of election, do come to, or believe in Christ; others do not come, do not believe; and the cause assigned is, because they are not of His sheep, because they are not given to Him. "All that the Father giveth Me shall come to Me" (John 6:37). Coming to Christ is believing on Him. "Ye believe not, **because** ye are not of My sheep" (John 10:26). "As many as were ordained to eternal life believed" (Acts 13:48). We may not (according to the Arminian notion) read it, "as many as believed were ordained unto life;" for this would be setting the cart before the horse, as if the means were ordained before the end. We are predestinated that we should be holy, not because we are holy (Eph. 1:4). We are foreordained to walk in good works, not because we do so (Eph. 2:10). We are predestinated to be conformed to the image of Christ, not because we are so (Rom. 8:29). It is the election that obtains faith, and not faith that obtains election (Romans 11:7). And the Apostle, in 2 Tim. 1:9, excludes all works (both foreseen and existing), showing that God's gracious purpose is the original of all. Yea, Paul himself was chosen that he might know the will of God, not that he was foreseen to do so (Acts 22:14); and he tells the Thessalonians, that "God hath from the beginning chosen you to salvation **through** sanctification of the Spirit and belief of the truth" (2 Thess. 2:13). We may not make that an antecedent to election which is but the consequent thereof. "I have chosen you, and ordained you, that ye should go and bring forth fruit" (John 15:16).

6. That which sets up an inferior cause because a superior ought not be admitted, and the conditional decree doth so.

God is the cause of causes, and the first cause of all things. There can be no being but from Him, there can be nothing before Him. "Of Him, and through Him, and to Him, are all things" (Rom. 11:36). "In Him we live, and move, and have our being" (Acts 17:28). O Lord, "Thou hast created all things, and for Thy pleasure they are and were created" (Rev. 4:11).

God is the chief efficient cause, and the ultimate end of all beings; but if any being be antecedent to the determinations of God's will, this would take away the dignity of the supreme cause, and make an act of man superior to that of God.

7. That which takes away the certainty and unchangeableness of the Divine decree ought not to be received, and the conditional decree doth so.

If anything in man move God to choose man, then the purpose of God cannot remain firm, but must depend on some contingent act in man, be it faith, works or perseverance. If it depends on our persevering in faith, it cannot be firm and certain, according to the Arminian doctrine of falling away; for the Arminian doctrine of falling away; for the Arminian hypothesis states the decree of God after this changeable dress, viz., "I will save **all** if they will obey Me; but I see they will sin. I must permit them, but I will condemn them all; yet this decree of condemnation shall not be peremptory. I will send Christ to redeem all, to save all again, if they will believe; but I see they will not. I will decree to save such as **I foresee** will believe, and persevere in believing." Oh what a changeable picture of an unchangeable God!

8. That which makes us to choose God, before God chooses us, ought not to be received; and

the conditional decree upon faith foreseen doth so.

If God does not choose us until faith is foreseen in us, then it necessarily follows that we choose God before He chooses us, and we love Him before He loves us, contrary to these scriptures, "Ye have not chose Me, but I have chosen you" (John 15:16). "We love Him, because He first loved us" (I John 4:19). But the Arminians go further still, for they say, "We must be foreseen, not only to believe, but also to persevere in believing;" that is, not only to choose God for our God, but also to continue in that choice to the last moment of our existence before we can be fit objects of God's choice or election!

9. That which taketh away the mysteriousness of the Divine decree ought to be rejected, and this doctrine of foreseen faith doth so.

It is a dangerous presumption for men to take upon themselves, with unwashed hands, to unriddle the deep mysteries of God with their carnal reason; where the great apostle stands at the gaze, crying, "O the depth, how unsearchable!" and "Who knoweth the mind of the Lord!" Had Paul been of the Arminian persuasion he would have answered, "Those are elected that are foreseen to believe and persevere!" This answer would not have been hard to understand even by the unlearned (that is, the carnal) men of the world, who "wrest the Scriptures unto

44

their own destruction." (2 Pet. 3:16). But Paul was ignorant, and these men are wiser than the Holy Ghost; for he tells us that our election proceedeth from the will of the Elector, and not from anything in the elected. The sovereign will of God is the supreme rule of all righteousness; He will have "mercy on whom He will have mercy, and whom He will He hardeneth" (Rom. 9:18). Had foreseen faith and perseverance been the causes and conditions of election, there had been no mystery in it.

10. That election which is shadowed out to us in God's love to Jacob (both **person** and **nation**) is the election according to truth; but that election was not upon foreseen faith or works.

First, Jacob the **person**. He was under electing love; all foresight of faith and works being excluded. "Jacob have I loved" (Rom. 9:12, 13). To love Jacob is to will unto him the greatest good, even everlasting salvation, and all things which accompany the same; and this was before there was any difference between him and Esau, for they were both alike in the womb, both conceived in sin. "For the children being not yet born, neither having done any good or evil, that the purpose of God according to **election** might stand, **not of works,** but of him that calleth; It was said unto her, The elder shall serve the younger" (Rom. 9:11, 12).

Second, Jacob, the **nation**. Our Election is typified by God's election of Israel, which plainly appears not to be an election upon foresight of worthiness in Israel; "Not for thy righteousness, or for the uprightness of thine heart . . . Understand therefore, that the Lord thy God giveth thee not this good land to possess it for thy righteousness; for thou art a **stiffnecked** people" (Deut. 9:5, 6). All works and worthiness are excluded, and the reason assigned is, "Because the Lord **loved** you" (Deut. 7:8).

11. That which sets up the rotten Dagon of man's freewill, before or above the ark of God's special predestinating grace, ought to be rejected; and the conditional decree doth so.

The conditional decree is grounded upon a foresight of our wills receiving or rejecting of proposed grace; and so man's will is made the first mover and advanced above God's will: and the act of predestination is put in the will and power of the predestinated, and not in that of the Divine Predestinator. Hereby the power of ordering man's salvation is wrested (as it were) out of God's hand's, and put into the hands of our freewill. Then salvation is the work of the **saved**, and not of the **saver**; and to **will** and to **do** is not of God's good pleasure (Phil. 2:13). Thus men wickedly think that God is such a one as themselves (Psa. 50:21), wavering and fluctuating in His counsels and hanging in **pen-**

dulous suspenses; yea, taking up new consultations, as dependent on the will of men, and the contingent acts flowing therefrom.

12. That which inferreth a succession of acts in God ought not to be admitted, and election upon foresight doth so.

God is **one act**, and in Him there can be no succession, for then He would not be "I AM." Foresight of faith necessarily presupposes a foregoing decree concerning the being of that faith foreseen. For, first, God must decree faith to be; second, He foresees that faith; third, then decrees to save upon that foresight. So that this foresight necessarily comes between two decrees.

Much more might be added, such as—foreseen faith can have no place in dying infants, yet of such is the kingdom of heaven, and their names are written in the book of life (see Rev. 20:12). But to sum up the whole in one sentence: **A conditional decree makes a conditional God, seeing the decree is God Himself decreeing.** Therefore it must be rejected.

"May not the Sovereign Lord on high
Dispense **His** favors as He will;
Choose some to life, while others die,
And yet be just and gracious still?

Shall man reply against the Lord,
And call his Maker's ways unjust?

47

The thunder of whose dreadful word
Can crush a thousand worlds to dust.

But, O my soul, if truths so bright
Should dazzle and confound thy sight,
Yet still His written will obey,
And wait the great decisive day!''

Objections Against the Absolute Decree of Predestination Answered

I have stated and proved the doctrine of absolute Divine Predestination. I have also considered, and, I trust, scripturally refuted the Arminian's notion thereof, that it is conditional. I shall now, thirdly, answer a few of the principal objections brought by them against this Divine absolute decree of unconditional predestination.

The Arminians deal with this doctrine as the heathen emperors did with primitive christians in the ten first persecutions, who wrapped them up in the skins of beasts, and then exposed them to be torn to pieces by their fierce ban-dogs; so do the Arminians with this great truth. They first dress it up in an ugly shape, with their own false glosses upon it, and then they let fly at it one cynical sarcasm after another, saying, "This doctrine of absolute predestination goes to accuse and charge God with injustice, dissimulation, hypocrisy,'' etc., etc.

Objection 1. Of injustice, in giving to equal persons unequal things; contrary to that scripture which saith, "that God is no respector of persons" (Acts 10:34).

Answer 1. This was objected against Paul's doctrine, "What shall we say then? is there unrighteousness (is there injustice) with God? God forbid" (Rom. 9:14). And seeing the apostle brings it in as the cavil of carnal reason against God's decree, we have therefore sufficient ground to reject it. God must not lose the honor of His righteousness, because the reason of it appears not to our shallow understandings. We may not reprehend what we cannot comprehend. The justice of God must not be measured by the standard of our reason; what is this but speaking wickedly for God, and talking deceitfully for Him (Job 13:7), and plainly robbing Him of all righteousness that is not consonant with our model? The work of God, and the wisdom of God, must ever be viewed as inseparably united.

2. God is righteousness itself; and darkness may sooner come from the sun (which is the fountain and source of light) than any unrighteous act from God. God's ways are always equal, though men think otherwise of them. "Yet ye say, The way of the Lord is not

49

equal. Hear now, O house of Israel; Is not My way equal? are not your ways unequal?'' (Ezek. 18:25); and though they be sometimes secret and past finding out (Rom. 11:33), yet are they always just. God's will is the rule ruling; but not as regulated by man's depraved reason. God is the origin of all good; He is also the Fountain of justice and equity. God is too kind to do us harm, and too just to do us wrong.

3. Jacob and Esau were equal in the womb, yet had an unequal disposing decree concerning them; this was God's right and power to do. This the apostle demonstrates, first, from Moses' testimony, ''I will make all My goodness pass before thee, and I will proclaim the name of the Lord before thee, and will be gracious to whom I will be gracious, and I will show mercy on whom I will show mercy'' (Ex. 33:19). It is His right to do so. And, secondly, from the example of the potter, who hath power over his pots, yet less than God over His creatures. Now that which the pot cannot do with the potter, that man may not do with his Maker. But the pot (supposing it could speak) could not blame the potter of injustice in appointing equal lumps to unequal ends.

4. God's decree is not an act of injustice, but of lordship and sovereignty. Justice always presupposes debt; but God (who was perfect in Himself from all eternity) could not be a debtor

to man, who had his all from God; the decree is not a matter of right and wrong, but of free favor; grace is God's own, He may do what He will with it. "Is it not lawful for Me to do what I will with Mine own? Is thine eye evil, because I am good?" (Matt. 20:15). If He give grace to some and not to others, it is no wrong in Him that is not bound to give it any.

5. God is not a respecter of persons, because He doth not choose men for their works' sake. It was before Jacob and Esau had done either good or evil. He finds all alike, and nothing to cast the balance of His choice but His own mere good pleasure. God is a free agent, and under no law in giving grace.

Objection 2. Of cruelty; as if God were worse to His creatures than tigers to their young: than rat-catchers who stop up all holes, and then hunt them with their dogs, etc., etc.

Answer 1. This is charging God foolishly, seeing no act of God can be a means to damn men. Men's own acts are the cause thereof; to wit, the fulfilling their own lusts. As reprobation gives not such a grace as infallibly to make them better, so it works nothing in them whereby they are made worse.

2. 'Tis a mere fallacy: as if the decree of non-election was the procuring cause of man's damnation. **Sin** is the cause of damnation, but reprobation is **not** the cause of sin. David's order

to Solomon concerning Joab and Shimei was not the cause why either the one or the other came to an untimely end; but it was treason against Solomon in Joab, and running from Jerusalem in Shimei, which procured their deaths (see I Kings 2:5, 28, 40, 42).

3. It is a false hypothesis to suppose that God, in the decree of reprobation, doth by as effectual means intend to bring men to damnation as in the decree of election to bring others to salvation: for salvation is a favour not due any, so God may absolutely give or deny it; but damnation is a punishment, so hath relation to a fault. Means to salvation is the gift of free grace, but damnation comes of man's own voluntary sin, and is the fruit or wages thereof. "The wages of sin is death; but the gift of God is eternal life through Jesus Christ our Lord" (Rom. 6:23). It is God that fitteth Peter for salvation; but Judas fits himself for damnation.

4. Should God constrain the creature to sin, and then damn him for it, He delighteth in the destruction of His creature, contrary to Ezek. 13:23 and 23:11. God did not thrust Adam into his sin, as, after he had willingly sinned, He thrust him out of Paradise. Man's punishment is from God as a judge; but man's destruction is from himself as a sinner. Let it be repeated, and again repeated, that man's sin came freely from himself.

Objection 3. It is objected against the absolute decree, that it makes God guilty of dissimulation in calling upon such as are under the negative part thereof to repent, etc., just as if God bid men, whose eyes He had closed, to judge of colours; or those whose feet He had bound, to rise up and walk.

Answer 1. The non-elects not repenting is not only from want of power ["No man can come to Me, except the Father . . . draw him" (John 6:44)]; but also from want of will, "Ye will not come to Me, that ye might have life" (John 5:40). None are damned because they can do no better, but because they will do no better. If there were no **will** there would be no **hell**: and this will be the very **hell of hells**, that men have been, felo de se, self destroyers.

2. Man had a power in Adam. God gave him knowledge in his understanding, rectitude in his will, and purity in his affections: these are all lost by the Fall. God must not lose His authority to command because man by reason of sin hath lost his ability to obey.

3. May it not more truly be said, that it is the Arminians who charge God with folly and dissumulation, by their representing Him as disappointed in His purpose, and by their bringing Him in as speaking thus: "I do indeed earnestly desire to save you, but ye so hinder that I cannot do what I desire; I would, if ye would:

therefore seeing I am, by you, frustrated of My intention, I will change My purpose of saving you, and My consequent will shall be a determination to destroy you?" So said Vorstius the Arminian, "Things may happen that may bring God to grief, having tried all things in vain!"

4. But there is another view to be taken here. When God giveth command to spiritual acts He granteth power to obey the same. So it was when Christ bade the man to stretch out the withered hand, and Lazarus to come forth out of the grave. The call and command of God is the conduit-pipe of strength and ability.

Objection 4. God's decree cannot be absolute and infallible, because it might have been frustrated by the possibility of Adam's standing.

Answer 1. Adam's standing was possible respecting himself, but not respecting God. To say that Adam might not have sinned is a categorical and simple proposition, and will hold good, Adam being considered in himself as clothed with the freedom of his will; and to say also, that it could not be but that Adam would sin is equally true, considering Adam was subordinate to the decree of God, determining what Adam would do out of the freedom of his own will.

2. As it respects man, Adam might have stood as well as fallen; for God gave not His creature a

law only, but also furnished him with power sufficient to keep that law if he would; and if man had not been mutable, he had been God and not man. Man is mutable, he had been God and not man. Man is mutable; God alone is immutable; in this He, the Lord, is distinguished from all created beings. Yet as it respects God, it was not possible man should stand; for in God's decree it was certain that man, being left to the mutability of his own will (upon Satan's tempting and God's permitting), would voluntarily incline to evil. Therefore Adam sinned freely in respect of himself, but necessarily in respect of God. He acted as freely therein as if there had been no decree, and yet as infallibly as if there had been no liberty. God's decree took not away man's liberty; man in the Fall, while fulfilling the decree of God, yet freely exercised the proper motions of his will.

3. Thus then God, by decreeing Adam's sin, did not subtract from Adam any grace that he had; for He decreed that he should sin voluntarily. He diminished not that power with which he was endued, only He superadded not that grace whereby Adam would infallibly not have fallen; which grace was no way due to man, neither was God bound to bestow it on him. So that Adam might stand, in respect of himself; yet certainly fall, in respect of God. The Jews might have

broken Christ's bones, in respect of their own free will in such actions, yet was it not possible they should do so; for "A bone of Him shall not be broken" (John 19:36). It was possible, in a sense, that Christ should be delivered from His passion by legions of angels (Matt. 26:53), "But how then shall the scriptures be fulfilled, that thus it **must** be?" (54). It was possible, in respect of the thing, that God might have pardoned sinners without a Christ; but impossible, inasmuch as God had decreed Christ to be the ransom. To argue on the Arminian hypothesis of freewill, 'tis possible none may be saved or none lost; and then either heaven or hell would be superfluous.

Objection 5. The predestinarians cannot agree about stating their decree; some stating it before the Fall, as the **supra-lapsarians;** and others after the Fall, as the **sub-lapsarians.**

Answer 1. The Arminians, by the law of retaliation, may be called sub-mortuarians, for their holding no full election till men die; and post-destinarians, for placing the eternal decree behind the race of man's life. Surely when believers die they are the subjects of glorification, not of election. Christ should have said (upon this hypothesis) to the penitent thief, "This day thou shalt be **fully elected** ," not, "Thou shalt be with Me in Paradise." And may they not also be styled re-lapsarians, for saying that the elect may totally and finally fall away;

and that he who is a child of God to-day may be a child of the devil to-morrow?

2. Those notions of **sub** and **supra** are but human conceptions of the order of the Divine decree, which so far transcends our understanding, that our weak capacities cannot comprehend it but after the manner of men. Those several states of man, before and after the Fall, are not in the Divine understanding as they are in ours, by a succession of acts, one after another; but God by one single act orders all things; and the Divine idea in the decree is a representative of all those states at once. They are not **subordinanda** but **co-ordinanda**; not this after that, but altogether in one instant of eternity.

Objection 6. Absolute election makes men remiss in duty; saying, "What need or use is there of good works? Let me live as I list; if I am elected to salvation I shall certainly be saved."

Answer 1. God's decree establishes means; it doth not only ordain the end, but the means to that end; and the one is never separated from the other. God decrees that the earth shall be fruitful; this doth not exlude, but includes, that the sun must shine upon it, showers must water it, and the husbandman must till it, as his God instructs him (Isa. 28:26). God decrees that fifteen years shall be added to Hezekiah's life; this made him neither careless of his health nor negligent of his food; he said not, "Though I run into the fire, or into the water, or drink poison, I shall nevertheless live so long;" but natural providence, in the due use of means, co-wrought so as to bring him on to that period of time pre-ordained for him. Man's industry is subservient to God's decree; it is called, "the life of thine hand" (Isa. 57:10). We may not tempt the Lord our God.

2. The golden chain has so linked the means to the end, and sanctification in order to salvation, that God doth infallibly stir up the elect to the use of the means, as well as bring them to the end by the means. "Brethren beloved of the Lord, God hath from the beginning chosen you to salvation, through **sanctification** of the spirit and belief of the truth" (2 Thess. 2:13). "A new heart also will I give you, and a new spirit will I put within you: and I will take away the stony heart out of your flesh, and I will give you a heart of flesh. And I will put My spirit within you, and **cause** you to walk in My statutes, and ye shall keep My judgments, and do them . . . Then shall ye remember your own evil ways, and your doings that were not good, and shall loathe yourselves in your own sight for your iniquities and for your abominations" (Ezek. 36:25-31). Those in whom the Lord hath put His Spirit, let them live as the list, and I am very sure they will live godly lives.

3. The Arminian eternal prescience infers as absolute a certainty, and necessity of events, as our predestination doth; for things must be foreordained to be before they can be foreseen that they shall be. Men may argue thus from their ground, "If I be eternally foreseen to believe, I shall believe and be saved." And yet on the contrary they teach men to say, "I can repent when I will; I may be elected whenever I please, though at present am living in lewdness, for I have a free will to repent even on my death-bed, so I may be saved if I think proper." **This is the doctrine that will make men remiss in duty!** But, for an elect soul, by the operation of the Holy Spirit, to read the heart of his covenant God towards him as loving him everlastingly, absolutely, and peculiarly; and, in consequence of His everlasting unchangeable love, bestowing on him, and giving for him, His greatest, His best gift, even Jesus Christ; let him live as he listeth, this will be his language, aye and his practice also, "For to me to live is Christ, and to die is gain." I love Thee, because Thou hast first loved me; I am constrained thereto by the all-powerful influences of Thy grace; this fleeting world can now afford nothing satisfactory to me. I shall never be satisfied till I am absent from the body and present with the Lord, till I awake with Thy likeness (Phil. 1:21; I John 4:19; 2 Cor. 5:14, 15; Psa. 17:15).

Objection 7. The doctrine of absolute reprobation makes men desperate; "Let me do what I can, if I am to be damned I shall be damned: I am under a fatal necessity."

Answer 1. This is to suck poison out of a sweet flower; to dash against the Rock of ages; to stumble at the Word, whereunto they were appointed (I Pet. 2:8). Why hath God ordered all things by an absolute decree for ever? It is "that men should fear before Him" (Eccl. 3:14). God acteth freely, as the first cause; and man freely, as the second; in concurrence and not by constraint.

2. This objection is well answered in the 17th Article of the Church of England: "For curious and carnal persons taking the spirit of Christ to have continually before their eyes the sentence of God's predestination, is a most dangerous downfall, whereby the devil doth thrust them either into desperation or into wretchedness of most unclean living, no less perilous than desperation."

3. No man may judge himself a reprobate in this life, and so grow desperate; for final disobedience (the only infallible evidence of reprobation) cannot be discovered till death. We are not to question the secret will of God but to pay attention to His revealed will.

4. The Arminian doctrine [God foresaw what good courses I would take of my freewill, so did

elect me] is miserable comfort to one whose heart is privy to myriads of departures from God. It was well said by the Psalmist, "Who can understand his errors?" Who can tell how oft he offendeth?" "Cleanse Thou me from secret faults" (Psa. 19:12).

To tell men (as Arminians do) that they may be justified and sanctified, and God's children, all but glorification; and yet, after this, may become rebrobates, and be damned in the end, is desperate doctrine indeed. Truly it is theirs which is the desperate doctrine; whereas our doctrine is only liable to false inferences from carnal persons—from such persons as drew false conclusions from our Lord's words, and said, "Who then can be saved?" (Luke 18:26). Such inferences are not fairly deduced, but corrupt consequences drawn from good premises.

"God's ways are just, His counsels wise,
No darkness can prevent His eyes;
No thought can fly, nor thing can move,
Unknown to Him that sits above.

He in the thickest darkness dwells,
Performs His work, the cause conceals,
But though His methods are unknown,
Judgment and **Truth** support His throne.

In heaven, and earth, and air, and seas,
He executes His firm decrees;
And by His saints it stands confess'd,
That what He does is ever best.

Wait then, my soul, submissive wait,
Prostrate before **His awful seat,**
And, midst the terrors of His rod,
Trust in a wise and gracious God.''

CHAPTER II.

OF UNIVERSAL REDEMPTION

Universal redemption, or, that Christ died for all men, cannot be a Gospel truth, because of the following arguments and reasons.

1. God the Father's election, God the Son's redemption, and God the Holy Ghost's sanctification, must all be of equal extent and latitude; but universal redemption, in the Arminian sense thereof, makes these unequal.

This is clear; for as the Father, Word, and Spirit are One in essence, so are they One in willing, working, and witnessing the redemption of sinners. As there are Three that bear witness on earth, the Spirit, the water, and the blood; so there are Three which bear record in heaven, the Father, the Word, and the Holy Ghost; ''and these Three agree in one'' (I John 5:6, 8). Whom the Father elects, the Son redeems, and the Holy Ghost sanctifies. If then there be a universal redemption there must be a universal election, and a universal sanctification also, and so, by consequence, a **universal salvation**. That the Son redeems no more than the Father elects is evident from two scriptures. The first is John 5:23, which declares the Son must be honoured as equal with the Father; but, to say that the Son redeemed all, and the Father elected but few, is to give greater honour to the One than to the Other, and to make an inequality in Their operations. The second scripture is John 17:9, 10: "All Thine are Mine and all Mine are Thine," etc. They were the Father's by electing love, and they became the Son's by gift and redemption: "Thine they were, and Thou gavest them Me" (v. 6). Christ redeems only those whom the Father gave unto Him. Hence God's "book of life" wherein the number of the elect is recorded, is called also the "Lamb's book of life;" intimating that the number of those elected by the Father is commensurate with those redeemed by the Son. That Christ redeems no greater number than the Spirit sanctifies is evident from I John 5:6, 7; there must be water to sanctify where there is blood to redeem. Christ's oblation is not of larger extent than the Spirit's operation. Thus it is most apparent that all the three Persons in the Trinity have one object and one design of love. They are equal in essence, equal in honour, and equal in operation.

2. The benefits of Christ's death and resurrection are of equal extent in their objects; but the benefit of Christ's resurrection is not extended to all.

That the benefit of Christ's resurrection is not extended to all and every one alike, but is peculiar to believers, is acknowledged even by the Arminians. That the death and resurrection of Christ are of equal extent in their objects is evident from Rom. 8:33, 34 (they are both put together), "Who shall lay anything to the charge of God's elect," for whom Christ died? Who can condemn those for whom Christ was raised? Those for whom Christ died and rose again cannot be condemned. "Who was delivered for our offences, and was raised again for our justification" (Rom. 4:25). Those that have the fruit of Christ's battle have the fruit of His victory also; but this cannot be said of all men, for one some the wrath of God abideth (John 3:36).

3. The benefit of Christ's death and intercession are of equal extent in their objects; but Christ intercedeth not for all.

This is expressly declared in Scripture: "I pray not for the world, but for them which Thou hast given Me; for they are Thine" (John 17:9). "They are not of the world" (John 17:14). Christ's intercession is "not for the world" at large, but only for those whom His Father hath given Him; and reason confirms this, for if Christ interceded for Judas, Pilate, etc., then had He a repulse, and was not always heard of the Father; contrary to John 11:42. Again, Christ is a High Priest, and the two parts of His priestly office, oblation and presentation, cannot be separated: and they which have a part in the former have part in the latter also. For the presentation doth necessarily imply the oblation, and gives a perpetual force thereto in the sight of God. (Heb. 9:12). Christ must intercede on the behalf of those whom He hath reconciled to God by His death; and His intercession is a personal presenting of Himself to His Father on behalf of those whom He personated on the Cross. We cannot say that there be some for whom Christ offered Himself upon earth but doth not intercede for in heaven; this would make Christ but a half-priest to some, and therefore not a faithful High Priest, contrary to sundry scriptures, Isa. 53:11, 12; I John 2:1, 2; Heb. 9:11, 12, and 10:19-21.

4. Those for whom Christ died have Christ for their surety; but all have not Christ for a surety.

All are sinners: and every sinner must die, either in himself or his Surety, for "the wages of sin is death." And the suretyship of Christ consists of this, that He died for us (Rom. 6:23). He was "made of curse for us," that is, in our stead (Gal. 3:13; 2 Cor. 5:21). Judah was surety for Benjamin's safety (Gen. 44:32), and Christ is the surety of the new covenant (Heb. 7:22); He took upon Him our sins in His death (Isa. 53:4-8; I Pet. 2:24). If Christ was a surety for all, then He offered up a satisfaction for all, in becoming sin, and bearing the curse and wrath of God in their stead. But this is not done for all; for Christ knows not workers of iniquity, and of them He says, "I never knew you" (Matt. 7:23); yet He knows His sheep, and He laid down His life for them (John 10:11-15).

5. If the covenant of grace be not to all, then Christ died not for all.

Christ's blood is called "the blood of the covenant" (Heb. 9:20), and "the blood of the New Testament" (Matt. 26:28). That the covenant of grace is not extended to all is evident, for it is made with the house of Israel only. "This shall be the covenant that I will make with the house of Israel after those days; saith the Lord, I will put My law in their inward parts, and write it in their hearts; and will be their God, and they shall be My people" (Jer. 31:33). The covenant is with those only in whose hearts the conditions are effectually wrought, to wit, putting God's fear therein, and writing His law in their minds, which the election only obtains. None dare say that God entered into covenant of grace with the "seed" of the serpent, but only with those whose "heel" the serpent hurteth (Gen. 3:15).

6. If Christ died for His sheep, His friends, and His church only, then He died not for all.

This is plain from several scriptures. "The good Shepherd giveth His life for the sheep . . . (I) know My sheep, and am known of Mine . . . and I lay down My life for My sheep" (John 10:11-15). "Greater love hath no man than this, that a man lay down his life for his friends. Ye are My friends" (John 5:13, 14). "Feed the church, which He hath purchased with His own blood" (Acts 20:28). "Christ loved the church, and gave Himself for it" (Eph. 5:25). Christ died for such as were Paul and Titus, not such as were Pharoah and Judas, who were "goats" and not "sheep" (Matt. 25:33). He died to save "His people from their sins," and therefore His name was called Jesus (Matt. 1:21); who are called the "redeemed of the Lord" (Psa. 107:2). Now seeing those for whom Christ died are such as "hear His voice and follow Him," to whom He "gives eternal life" (John 10:27, 28), such as He sanctifies, and cleanses, and presents to Himself "without spot or wrinkle" (Eph. 5:27), and such as He hath "redeemed from all iniquity, to purify them to Himself a peculiar people" (Titus 2:14), such as are His people, His chosen, His children, it cannot be intended for all unless we say that Pharoah, Judas, etc., were of the sheep, friends, and church of Christ. It is true He died for enemies (Rom. 5:10), but it was to reconcile them to God; such were the believing Romans, who being Gentiles, Christ called "other sheep," not of the Jewish fold.

7. Those for whom Christ's death was intended, to them it must be applied; but it is not applied to all, therefore it was not intended for all.

The end and design cannot be severed from the action to accomplish that end. Christ's aim being to bestow what He obtains, He obtains nothing but what He applies. He Himself speaks of some from whom the gospel was hid, and of others to whom it was revealed or made known. "Thou hast hid these things from the wise and prudent, and hast revealed them unto babes" (Matt. 11:25). The sum total of the intercession of Christ is, that what He has obtained may be applied, (see John 17 throughout).

8. If Christ died for all, then must all be reconciled to God; but all are not reconciled.

Sin hinders reconciliation; and Christ's death is a propitiation for sin (Rom. 3:25), so that all for whom Christ died must be reconciled to God; the death of Christ is the cause, and reconciliation the effect following the cause. If all be reconciled, all must be saved, and nothing can be laid to the charge of any. Take away the sin, and you acquit the sinner. But to grant such an acquitance and reconciliation to all brings in many absurdities; for upon this hypothesis it follows, 1st that Cain, Pharaoh etc., were reconciled to God by Christ's death when they were (at the time of Christ's dying) in the torments of hell, and never to be delivered therefrom. 2nd, that God damns reconciled persons. 3rd, that God takes double pay for one fault, in punishing both the Surety and the debtor. 4th, that Christ's reconciling of some is ineffectual, etc. But these things are not so; for to those for whom Christ died repentance is granted, and remission of sins (Acts 5:31); to them is given freedom from the slavery of sin, and regeneration to newness of life (Rom. 6:6; Heb. 2:14, 15); on them is bestowed purifying grace, ''purifying their hearts by faith'' (Acts 15:9); they have the blood of Christ to purge their conscience from dead works, that they may serve the living God (Heb. 9:14), and theirs is life eternal: ''I give to them eternal life, and they shall never perish'' (John 10:28). All these fruits are evidences of our reconciliation by Christ's death.

9. That cannot be a truth which the Scripture nowhere affirms; and it nowhere asserts that Christ died for all men, much less for every man individually; therefore it is not a truth.

It is true Christ is said to ''give His life a ransom for all;'' but not for all men, or for every man individually; the Scripture is the best expounder of itself, and the ''all'' is rendered ''many'' in Matt. 20:28, and Mark 10:45: ''The Son of man came to give His life a ransom for many.'' ''My blood is shed for many, for the remission of sins'' (Matt. 26:28); and it is so frequently restrained to His sheep, friends, church, believers, chosen, and such as are given to Christ, that it must mean some of all sorts; which, in equivalent terms, is clearly expressed in Rev. 5:9, 10: ''Thou hast redeemed us out of every kindred and tongue, and people and nation.'' Therefore the word "all" must be taken for all the elect, all His church, all His children that the Father hath given Him, etc., not all men universally, and every man individually.

10. That which opposes the attributes of God ought not to be received; and universal redemption doth so.

1st. It opposes His justice. If Christ redeemed Pharaoh and Judas, then redeemed souls are unjustly damned; this hypothesis sets the death of Christ in direct opposition to God's justice. And how could Christ die for Judas's sin when Christ's death was his very sin?

2nd. It opposes His wisdom. As if God should love and hate the same person at the same time; Esau must be loved if Christ is given to die for him, yet hated, as being ordained to death from all eternity.

3rd. It opposes His power. If Christ died intentionally (as to God) for all, then God's intentions are frustrated, seeing all are not saved. Then is God not omnipotent if crossed in His designs by the work of His own hands. And to say that freedom was obtained by Christ's death for those who are not set free is ridiculous, and making a laughing stock of religion.

Objections Against Particular Redemption Answered.

Objection 1. What every one is bound to believe must be true, and it is the duty of all men to believe; therefore Christ must have died for all men.

Answer 1. Suppose we grant this position, would not the doctrine of discriminating love be thereby destroyed? Would it not be poor comfort for a distressed soul to believe that Christ died for it, no more than for Judas and all the damned in hell?

2. They to whom the Gospel never came, they who have never heard of the death of Christ, are not bound to believe that Christ died for them. What God reveals is true; but God nowhere reveals that it is His intention that Judas shall believe, or that all shall believe.

3. All have not the Gospel preached to them; and many to whom it is preached only hear the sound thereof with the outward ear: they come and go in an attendance thereon as the door upon its hinges, in a way of mere formality. They are not impressed with a sight and sense of their state as sinners. They are not weary and heavy laden because of sin. The proclamation by the gospel trumpet of redemption for sin through Christ's blood is not a joyful sound to them; they know not their need thereof. Evangelical repentance is the gift of free grace; faith is the gift of

God. What is God's, as a gift to bestow, cannot be man's duty to perform as a condition of salvation. Those who are invited to look to Christ, to come to Him for salvation, are very minutely described: they are the weary and heavy laden with sin, the penitent, the hungry and thirsty soul, etc., etc.; these are the characters invited to come to and believe in Christ, and not all men (Matt. 11:28; Isa. 55:1; Mark 2:17).

Objection 2. The words "all" and "every," often used in Scripture, must be taken universally.

Answer 1. "**All**" and "**every**" must not be taken for a universal affirmative collectively, and for every man individually, in the common quoted scriptures; but distributely, as in Matt. 9:35, where we are told that Christ went about healing every sickness and every disease among the people; that is, any and every kind of disease, for Christ healed not every disease individually. Also in Col. 1:28, where "every" is taken distributively three times over, and must be restricted to those to whom Paul preached.

2. "All" in I Tim. 2:4, cannot be taken for every man individually, since it is not the will of God that all men in this large sense should be saved: for it is His will that some men should be damned, and that very justly, for their sins and transgressions. Unto some men it will be said, "Depart, ye cursed, into everlasting fire." If

God willeth all men to be saved, then all men will be saved, for "He (God) doeth according to His will in the army of heaven, and among the inhabitants of the earth" (Dan. 4:35). God faileth not, He cannot be disappointed in His own will, for He worketh all things after the counsel thereof. Again, in Heb. 2:9, Jesus is said to "taste death for every man;" it is in the very next verse restricted to "sons brought to glory," and in ver. 11, to "sanctified" ones. I Tim. 2:6 ("who gave Himself a ransom for all") is rendered in the parallel text in Titus 2:14, "who gave Himself for us." Now, who are the persons called "us" in this text? Are they not particularized as "redeemed from all iniquity, purified and made a peculiar people?" For "all" of this description Christ gave Himself a ransom, and for none else.

The prophet David saith, "All men are liars;" take the word strictly, and he must be a liar that saith so.

Objection 3. In John 3:16, and in I John 2:2, it is declared that God gave Christ for the "world," and for the sins of the "whole world;" which must be taken literally.

Answer 1. The word "world" is of various significations. A decree went out that "all the world should be taxed" (Luke 2:1), that is, the Roman empire and such countries in subjection thereto. The faith of the church of Rome was "spoken of throughout the whole world" (Rom. 1:8), that is, throughout all the churches, and among all the saints in the world. When the Pharisees said of Christ, "Behold, the world is gone after Him" (John 12:19), by reference we find that they meant "much people" who went out of Jerusalem to meet Jesus, crying, "Hosanna" (vv. 12, 13). The Pharisees themselves, who so said, they were not gone after Christ; therefore the whole world was not gone, they themselves not being gone. So John 3:16: "God so loved the world" cannot be understood of the world in a strict sense, for so birds, beasts, fishes, and all inanimate things are comprehended, which cannot have everlasting life; nor can it be the world of men, but as God is the Preserver of both man and beast (Psa. 31:6). There is God's love to creatures, His love to men, and His love to good men. God's love was the cause of His sending Christ, and the word **"whosoever"** (in the verse) restrains this love of God to some and not to others. It must therefore be properly God's love to good men, the third love; not such as He found good, but such as He made so.

2. There is a world of **believers** (Rev. 5:9); and as manna was only for Israel, so Christ, the true manna, the Bread from heaven, gives life to the world of believers only (John 6:33). Christ was believed on in the world of believers only (I Tim. 3:16); the reconciled world (2 Cor. 5:19): and

"all men have not faith" (2 Thess. 3:2). There is also the world of unbelievers. "All the world wondered after the beast. And "they worshipped the dragon" (Rev. 13:3, 4). "The whole world lieth in wickedness" (I John 5:19). The believing world is a world in the world ("these are in the world," John 17:11); and they are taken and chosen **out** of the world. They are in the world, and sojourning among the inhabitants thereof as strangers and pilgrims only, this not being their rest, their home; their desires being towards a better country (Heb. 11:13-16). And that they are taken and chosen out of the world and given to Christ is clear from John 15:19: "If ye were of the world, the world would love his own; but because ye are not of the world, but I have chosen you out of the world, therefore, the world hateth you." Also from John 17:6, 9: "I have manifested Thy Name unto the men which Thou gavest Me out of the world . . . I pray for them; I pray not for the world."

"Zion's garden wall'd around,
Chosen and made peculiar ground;
A little spot, enclosed by grace,
Out of the world's wide wilderness."

3. It is granted that God hath a respect for all mankind. "We trust," saith Paul, "in the living God, who is the Saviour," i.e., the Preserver, "of all men, especially of those that believe" (I

Tim. 4:10). "The Lord is good to all, and His tender mercies are over all His works" (Psa. 145:9). "He maketh His sun to rise on the evil and on the good; and sendeth rain on the just and on the unjust" (Matt. 5:45). All this implies not eternal preservation, but only temporal providence and reservation; for the wages of sin would have been paid at the birth thereof, and the world (through confusion by sin) would have fallen about Adam's ears, had not Christ been the glorious undertaker.

All that are redeemed are redeemed by Christ; but the elect only are given to Him; they alone have an interest in Him, are redeemed by Him, and they shall be glorified with Him.

4. The word "world" is sometimes in Scripture put for Gentiles in opposition to Jews, and so it is in I John 1:2. John wrote to the Jews, and ministered unto the circumcision (see Gal. 2:9), and he says unto them, "Christ is the propitiation for our sins, and not for ours only, but also for the sins of the whole world," that is, not for the Jews only, but for the Gentiles also. The Jewish nation considered themselves as the peculiar people of God; and so they were, for to them "pertained the adoption, and the glory, and the covenants, and the giving of the law, and the service of God, and the promises." And Christ was a Jew, "of whom concerning the flesh Christ came" (Rom. 9:4, 5). The Jews were

always taught to appropriate the Messiah exclusively to themselves, to the utter rejection of the Gentiles, who were called "strangers," "uncircumcised," "common," "unclean," "dogs," etc. And it was unlawful for a Jew to keep company or have any dealings with a Gentile (see Matt. 10:5; Mark 7:17; Acts 10:28, and 11:3). The salvation of the Gentiles is in various parts of Scripture called a "mystery," "hidden mystery;" the "mystery of Christ which in other ages was not made known unto the sons of men . . . that the Gentiles should be fellow heirs" (Eph. 3:4-6; Col. 1:27). But when this mystery was revealed and made fully known by the divine mission to Paul, who was by Christ sent to preach to the Gentiles (Acts 26:17, 18), when it was declared by the vision of the unclean beasts and the Lord's consequent commission to Peter (Acts 6:9-15, 20), then the contentions of the circumcision ceased (Acts 11:2, 3); they found "the middle wall of partition" between Jew and Gentile was "broken down;" the latter, who before were "aliens from the commonwealth of Israel, and strangers to the covenants of promise," being now "brought nigh by the blood of Christ". They glorified God saying, "Then hath God also to the **Gentiles** granted repentance unto life." Jesus Christ is not only the propitiation for the sins of us **Jews,** but for the **Gentiles** also (Eph. 2:11-18).

5. The foregoing is proved from Rom. 11:12, where the two words, "world" and "Gentiles," are both used as signifying one and the same thing. "If the fall of them (Jews) be the riches of the world, and the diminishing of them the riches of the Gentiles; how much more their fulness?"

"It was a controversy agitated among the Jewish doctors whether, when the Messiah came, the Gentiles, the 'world' should have any benefit by Him; the majority was exceeding large on the negative of the question; only some few, as old Simeon and others, knew that He should be 'a light to lighten the Gentiles,' as well as 'the glory of His people of Israel.' The rest concluded that the most severe judgments and dreadful calamities would befall the Gentiles; yea, that they should be cast into hell, in the room of the Israelites" (Dr. John Gill).

Objection 4. Surely Christ hath as much efficacy to save as to damn (see Rom. 5:17).

Answer 1. There is a difference between a necessary extension and a voluntary one. Adam's sin was extensive necessarily, but salvation by Christ is of free grace, wholly of God's pleasure, and is therefore called the "free gift" (Rom. 5:15).

2. Christ is nowhere compared to Adam in the extent of His object, but only in the efficacy of His obedience. All, and every one, are not in

Christ radically, as they were in Adam; all are not given to Christ; but "as many (saith Christ) as Thou has given Me." As all the offspring of Adam fell by his sin, so all that are Christ's are saved by His death; as all that are in Adam die, so all that are in Christ are made alive (I Cor. 15:22).

3. That the apostle might not be misunderstood, and the word "all" in Rom. 5:18 taken universally, the term of comprehension is varied in the following verse, and "all" is rendered "many." "By the obedience of one shall many be made righteous."

Objection 5. In Rom. 14:15, it is said, "destroy not him for whom Christ died." And in 2 Pet. 2:1, persons are described as "denying the Lord that bought them."

Answer 1. Everlasting destruction cannot be intended by the word destroy in Rom. 14:15, and the context shows this; for the apostle, throughout the chapter, is exhorting the believing Romans not to contemn or condemn one another on account of things indifferent; neither to destroy the weak believer's peace of mind by doing any thing (which although it be indifferent, and not evil in itself) may yet prove a stumbling-block to him. I "am persuaded," says Paul, "that there is nothing unclean of itself; but to him that esteemeth anything unclean, to him it is unclean. If thy brother be grieved with thy meat, now walkest thou not charitably. Destroy not'' (by thy conduct in eating meat esteemed by thy brother unclean) the peace of mind of one of the weaklings of that flock ''for which Christ died.'' Put not a stumbling-block, or an occasion of falling or offence in thy weak brother's way (Rom. 14:13-15). ''Whether therefore ye eat, or drink, or whatsoever ye do, do all to the glory of God. **Give none offense**'' (I Cor. 10:31, 32). To the same purport is I Cor. 8 throughout.

2. The persons spoken of in 2 Pet. 2:1, as ''denying the Lord that bought them,'' are described by the apostle thus, **''false teachers''**—hypocritical professors, tares among the wheat (Matt. 13:25, 38), in whom was never the root of the matter; not bought and redeemed by Christ from eternal death, but had merely escaped, or abstained, from the pollutions of the world through a theoretical knowledge of the Lord and Saviour Jesus Christ (ver. 20). To answer certain purposes, they made an outward profession of the gospel, which obliged them for a space to be outwardly moral; associated with the people of God, insinuated themselves into churches, privily introduced therein damnable heresies; many followed their pernicious ways, by reason of whom the way of truth was evil spoken of, and they made merchandise of true believers; they continued thus for a while, and

then either their sheep's clothing was stripped off them, or they threw it off themselves, and returned back again into the world. They were all this while "goats" and not "sheep;" ravening wolves, not gentle lambs. And Peter closes the chapter concerning them by saying, "It is happened to them according to the true proverb. The dog is turned to its own vomit again, and the sow that was washed to her wallowing in the mire" (2 Pet. 2:1-3 and 17-22).

3. The apostle (2 Pet. 2:1) does not appear to be there speaking concerning the purchase of the Redeemer's blood—the name or title, Lord (Greek, **depotes**), is nowhere else applied to Christ in the New Testament, but to the Father, as in Luke 2:29; Acts 4:24; 2 Tim. 2:22; and especially in Jude 4, where "the only Lord God" is distinguished from "our Lord Jesus Christ." And even though it could be proved to apply to Christ in the above text, it may be explained upon the principle that it is no unusual thing with the inspired writers to speak of things not as they actually are, but according to the profession of the party. Thus, for instance, (Matt. 13:12): "Whosoever hath, to him shall be given, and he shall have more abundance; but whosoever hath not, from him shall be taken away even that he hath" that is, "which he seemeth to have," as explained in Luke 8:18. Thus apostates are said to be "twice dead," which would seem to im-

port that they had been spiritually alive, though in fact that was never the case, but merely what they professed to be.

4. So that, if we even grant the premises, it only follows that such as think themselves redeemed, or are thought so by others, may blaspheme and perish; yet this makes not all the world redeemed; this can by no means establish the doctrine of **Universal** Redemption.

CHAPTER III
OF FREE-WILL IN THE FALLEN STATE
AND OF EFFECTUAL VOCATION
OR CONVERSION TO GOD

The Arminians not only deny election to be an eternal, peculiar, unconditional, and irreversible act of God; and assert that Christ died equally and indiscriminately for every individual of mankind; for them that perish no less than for them that are saved; but they also aver that saving grace is tendered to the acceptance of every man; which he may or may not receive, just as he pleases. That the regenerating power of the Holy Spirit in conversion is not invincible but is suspended, or depends for its efficacy on the will of man. That notwithstanding Christ's death, it was possible (in respect of free-will) that all should perish; that now, by His death for all, true grace is given to all; which they may improve, hold fast, and be saved; or despise, neglect, cast away, and be lost!

The will of man is naturally a self-determining power and principle, but hath since the Fall the strong bias of sin upon it. Freedom is radically and originally in the will, not in the understanding; and it is an essential property of it, that it cannot be compelled by any created external agent, in its own free choice. Now it is no wonder, if many mistakes arise about this great engine of the Almighty, seeing the soul knows not itself but by reflection; and though we know its qualities and operations, yet we know not its essence.

Man is considered in a fourfold state:—I. The state of creation, therein he had free-will either to good or evil, but was necessitated to neither. 2. The state of degeneration, wherein he is a servant to sin, and necessitated to evil. 3. The state of regeneration, wherein he is freed from the slavery and dominion of sin, and from the love of sin, though not at present, from the inbred corruptions and inbeing thereof. 4. The state of glorification, wherein man is both freely and necessarily good, perfect, and happy. In the first estate, man is free; in the second, a slave; in the third, set free; and in the fourth, having a glorious liberty.

The controversy is concerning the second state, wherein we say, that man is under a necessity of sinning, yet free from coercion; he is free to evil, but not to good; which appears by the following arguments:

1. That there is no free-will to good in the fallen estate, is proved from the Fall itself; if man, in the Fall, lost his free-will to good, then it cannot be found in the fallen estate.

The Fall implies: The loss of that original righteousness and perfection wherein man was created. If the other faculties of the soul became

85

depraved, and were stripped of their primitive lustre by the Fall, then must the will also be a sharer in that depravation. Now the depravity of the will is proved by considering the good it hath lost, and the evil it hath gained, through Adam's sin. The good it has lost is sixfold: power, order, stability prudence, obedience, liberty. The evil it hath gained is a threefold rebellion: 1. Against the counsel of the mind. 2. Against the controls of conscience. 3. Against the commands of God. This king of the Isle of Man (the will), when he came first out of God's mint, was a curious silver-piece, and shone most gloriously; but now, being fallen among thieves, is robbed of all, hath ashes for beauty, and is a tyrant upon a dunghill; yea, is free from righteousness, but a very slave to sin (Rom. 6:17-20). Before the Fall, the will had liberty both to good or evil, to do or not to do; but since the Fall, the will is evil, only evil, and continually evil (Gen. 6:5). The whole heart now is evil extensively, only evil intensively, and continually evil protensively.

2. If conversion be a new creation, then fallen man hath not a free-will to good.

A convert is called a "new creature," or a "new creation" in Gal. 6:15, and 2 Cor. 5:17. Creation is a production of something out of nothing; but if there be a free-will to do good in man before conversion, then is there something of its own nature spiritually good in unconverted man towards the work of conversion; so can it not be called a new creature. Sure I am every experienced soul finds the contrary in that work; the whole frame is out of frame in the unconverted state; and man is a confused chaos, a vast emptiness, when this creating power comes upon him. Yea, a greater power is required to recreate this little world than at first to create the greater; for in this, though there be no preexisting good matter, yet is there resisting evil matter. The creation of the great world was the work of God's Word (Psa. 33:6); of His fingers (Psa. 8:3); or of His hands (Psa. 102:25). But to restore (the little world) **man,** requires God's arm (Luke 1:51); nay, Christ set His sides to it (Luke 22:44); it cost Him tears and agony and blood. New qualities and operations are created in us; the will to will well, and the power to do well, are ascribed to this creating almighty power in the effectual conversion of souls to God. ''It is God which worketh in you, both to will and to do of His good pleasure'' (Phil. 2:13).

3. If conversion be a new-begetting, or generation, then fallen man hath no free-will to good.

Generation is the motion to a being, and a proceeding into a being; this presupposes that there is no being before; for we are not, we are nothing before we be begotten; as it holds true in generation, so in regeneration: ''Of His own

87

will begat He us" (Jas. 1:18). It is not said that God begat us of our wills (yet this should be said were there in us a freewill to good) but of God's will; and till then we are not (I Cor. 1:28).

Unconverted men are nothing creatures. 1st. A natural nothing; for what is the great womb whence all things come but nothing? 2nd. A moral nothing; we are morally worse than nothing, that is miserable; "Man is vanity," or as in the Hebrew, Adam is abel, that is, vanity (Psa. 39:5); "and a lie" (Psa. 62:9). "The heart of the wicked is little worth" (Prov. 10:20); neither for use nor service; as a shadow is not useful for war, nor a statue for prayer, so fallen man is unfit for the service of God, for his best actions are sin. All this shows we are nothing, and have not a free-will to good, till begotten of God.

4. If conversion be a new birth, then fallen man hath not a free-will to good.

We cannot have a birth of ourselves; a babe cannot be born of itself; nothing can have its original from itself, for it would then be before and after itself; it would be and would not be, at the same time. Thus are we taught to look up above ourselves for our new birth. "Except a man be born again," or from above (John 3:3). We are born, not of the flesh, "but of the Spirit" (v. 6). Our first birth is of the earth, earthy; our second birth is from the Lord, heavenly; "Born of God" (I John 3:9).

5. If conversion be a quickening of one that is dead in sin, then fallen man hath no freewill to good.

This is proved from Eph. 2:1: "You hath He quickened who were dead" etc. He doth not say half dead, as the man was that fell among thieves (Luke 10:30); but wholly dead, as to spiritual life. There is no manner of good in us (Rom. 7:18). And "we are not sufficient of ourselves to think" a good thought till Christ quickens us (2 Cor. 3:5). "Without Him we can do nothing" (John 15:5). From Him is our fruit found (Hos. 14:8); both the bud of good desires, the blossom of good purposes, and the fruit of good actions. Aaron's rod (a dry stick without a root) is a fit emblem; it budded, blossomed, and brought forth almonds; this was not done by any inward principle or power of nature, but it was solely and wholly the work of God. So Ezekiel's dry bones were made to live; nothing of that life was from themselves, but all from God. Thus it is in this spiritual life; we can contribute nothing whereby to dispose ourselves to will that which is truly good; we cannot so much as call Christ Lord, but by the Spirit (I Cor. 12:3). If there be no life, but through union with Christ, then till we be engrafted into that blessed and bleeding vine we cannot bring forth fruit unto God. And it is not any natural power or principle in us that can engraft us into Christ, for faith is the engrafting grace, and that is "the gift of God" (Eph. 2:8), the grace whereby the just live (Hab. 2:4), and whereby Christ dwells in our hearts (Eph. 3:17). Till then we are dead, and have no free will to good.

6. If regeneration, or recovery from the state of degeneration, be a resurrection, then fallen man hath no free-will to good.

That regeneration is a resurrection is manifest from the following scriptures: "Verily, verily, I say unto you, the hour is coming, and now is, when the dead shall hear the voice of the Son of God: and they that hear shall live" (John 5:25). "When we were dead in sins, (He) hath quickened us together with Christ" and "hath raised us up" etc. (Eph. 2:5,6). It requires as much power to raise, quicken, and make alive a sinner dead in trespasses and sins, as to raise Christ from the dead, (Eph. 1:19,20). To raise up Christ, and to work faith in us, requires "the exceeding greatness of His power," (v. 19). Here are three gradations: power, greatness of power, and as if that were too little, the apostle adds, "according to the working of His mighty power." The original words imply not only a working, but an **effectual force** in working; such strength as in the arms of valiant men who can do great exploits. Nay more, it is beyond all this, it implies a power that can do all things, an omnipotent power. Surely, had there been an internal principle in us toward this great work, or any free-will in us to good, Paul would not have used those gradations, nor such emphatical, significant expressions. This work of regeneration would not then have required the effectual, forcible power of the valiant arm of God; even such a power as raised up Christ from the dead, whereby He was declared to be the Son of God (Rom. 1:4).

7. If moral persuasion be altogether insufficent of itself to recover man from his fallen state, then fallen man hath no free-will to do good.

If moral persuasion could recover man, then faith would be an easy work, and not require such mighty power as has just been proved. Christ did more to the raising of Lazarus than morally persuade him to come out of the grave; when Christ said, "Lazarus, come forth" (John 11:43) a mighty power went along with the command, which gave effect thereto. It is not enough to persuade a prisoner to come forth, but his chains must be struck off, and the prison doors must be opened (Acts 12:6,7, 10); and man is more than a mere prisoner; he is dead in sin, so must have a quickening grace; which moral persuasion can never accomplish.

8. If Christ be **All** in all (Col. 3:11), in matters of salvation, then man is nothing at all as to that

work, and hath not in himself a freewill to good.

First. Christ's work is to bore the ear, which before is stopped like the deaf adder's to the voice of the charmer (Psa. 58:4,5). Christ gives the understanding ear; "He openeth also their ear to discipline, and commandeth that they return from iniquity" (Job 36:10). See Psa. 40: 6, and Isa. 50:4, which passages, although spoken of Christ, hold good concerning His people.

Second. Christ opens not only the ear, but the heart also (Acts 16:14). The Lord opened the heart of Lydia, not she her own heart; which she might have done had she a freewill to good. The key of the heart hangs at Christ's girdle. "He that openeth and no man shutteth; and shutteth, and no man openeth" (Rev. 3:7). Moral persuasion will never prove effectual to open the heart of man.

Third. Besides Christ there is no Saviour (Isa. 43:11; Hosea 13:4); but freewill Arminianism makes man a **co-saviour** with Christ; as if there was a halving of it between the grace of Christ and the will of man, and the latter dividing the spoil with the former; yea, deserving the greater share: for if Christ be only a monitor, and persuade to good, then man's own will is the principal author of its own goodness; and he makes himself to differ from others, and hath something, that he received not at conversion, whereof to boast before God. "Who maketh thee to differ from another? and what hast thou that thou didst not receive? now if thou didst receive it, why dost thou **glory**, as if thou hadst **not** received it?" (I Cor. 4:7). Persuastion leaves the admonished will to its own indifferency, not changing it at all; so man becomes his own saviour, at least Christ is not the only Saviour; how then is Christ **all** in all?

9. If fallen man must be drawn to goodness, then hath he no free-will to good.

That moral persuasion will not bring a soul to Christ; that man cannot come himself, but must be drawn, is proved from John 6:44: "No man **can** come to Me, except the Father which hath sent Me draw him." Drawing is a bringing of anything out of its course and channel by an influence from without, and not from an inate power or principle from within. In Sol. Song 1:4, it is not said lead, but "draw;" in drawing there is less will and more power than in leading; and though God draws us strongly, yet He doth it sweetly. As we are drawn, we have not a free-will to good, else man fell in his understanding only, not in his will; yet are we volunteers (Psa. 110:3), a willing people; not that Christ finds us so, but makes us so "in the day of His power," and when He speaks to us with a strong hand (Isa. 8:11). We are naturally haters of God, and at enmity with Him (Rom. 1:30; 8:7), but the Spirit

93

gives a new power to the soul, and then acts and influences that power to good; so draws a God-hater to love Him. This is more than a bare persuasion to a stone to be **warm,** for God takes away the "heart of stone," and gives a "heart of flesh" (Ezek. 36:26). God the Spirit gives the inclination to come, and the very power of coming to Christ; and Christ finds nothing that is good in us (Rom. 7:18).

10. If the soul of man be passive in effectual vocation, then is there in fallen man no free-will to good.

The spirit of grace is compared to a precious liquor that is infused; and the called and chosen of God are styled vessels of mercy. "I will pour upon the house of David . . . the spirit of grace" etc. (Zech. 12:10); "the vessels of mercy prepared unto glory" (Rom. 9:23). Now a vessel is a passive receiver of liquor poured into it. "The love of God is shed abroad in our hearts by the Holy Ghost" (Rom. 5:5); that is, poured out and infused into God's vessels of mercy. The atmosphere is passive when it receives light, and Adam's body was passive when God inspired it with life; though it was formed and organized, yet was it lifeless and breathless (Gen. 2:7). So the will of man (in respect of this first reception of grace) hath neither concurrence nor cooperation active; the Lord is alone in that work. Apart from the influences of Divine grace, it is a very hell to any to be brought from hell; though it be an hell to us to stay after God hath opened our eyes and changed our hearts. Corrupt nature neither can nor will contribute anything to destroy its own corruptions. In the first work, the will moveth not itself, but is moved by God. The will, as a creature, must obey its Creator; yet as a sinful depraved will, it obeys not willingly till "made willing" (Psa. 110:3). Man, and the will of man, while in an unregenerate state, may be compared to the tied-up colt in Mark 11:2 (tied and bound with sin's chain), but when "the Lord hath need of him," and the "day of His power" is come, the sinner must then be loosed and let go.

11. To deny grace, irresistible special grace in conversion, is abominable; and the doctrine of freewill is a denial of this.

The advocates for freewill say, "If a man improves his naturals, God is bound to give him spirituals." What is this but turning grace into debt? And to say that the reason why one believes and another does not arises from the cooperation of the freewill of him that believeth, is to deny special irresistible grace as peculiar to the elect. All which is contrary to these scriptures: John 6:37, 45; Rom. 8:14; I Cor. 1:23, 24; I John 4:13, and very many others. God's dispensations towards His people are all of free grace. He quickens whom He will (John 5:21). The heart of one sinner is caused to melt as wax before the fire and receive God's seal, while the heart of another remains as immovable as marble, and as the rock that cannot be shaken; this is the work of God's gracious dispensation. "He hath mercy on whom He will have mercy, and whom He will He hardeneth" (Rom. 9:18). The Spirit blows where it listeth (John 3:8). God may drop in grace, even with the first breathings of life, and regenerate a babe as soon as it be brought forth; as John Baptist, who was filled with the Holy Ghost, even from his mother's womb (Luke 1:15). And others He may cast into the womb of the new birth when in the very act of dropping out of the world, at the eleventh, yea, at the twelfth hour, as the thief on the cross. Oh, who can order the ways of grace, and set bounds to the Spirit of God in its breathings on man!

12. Free-will brings with it so many absurdities that it cannot be received.

First. It makes man the cause of his own salvation.

Second. It puts grace into man's power, not man's will under the power of grace.

Third. It robs God of the honor of making one to differ from another, and ascribes it to man.

Fourth. It allows man a liberty of boasting to God, saying, "God, I thank Thee that Thou gavest me power to will (yet Thou gavest that to Judas as well as me), but I thank myself for the act of willingness, seeing I receive from Thee no more than Judas did."

Fifth. It exempts the creature from the power of God, as if man, spider-like, could spin a thread out of his own bowels whereon to climb to heaven.

Sixth. It maketh man the cause why God willeth this or that; so God must attend on the will of man, and not be infallible in His decrees, nor working all things according to the counsel of His own will (Eph. 1:11; Psa. 115:3).

Seventh. Then the apostle James lied in saying "every good gift" is from God (Jas. 1:17); and Paul also was mistaken in Rom. 9:11. He should have said, "It is of man that willeth and runneth," and not, "Of God that showeth mercy."

Objections in Favor of Free-Will Answered

Objection I. There is a law written in the hearts of fallen mankind (Rom. 2:15).

Answer I. This is conscience bearing witness of right and wrong (see the same verse). Impotency is in the **will**.

2. Adam begat a son "in his own image" (Gen. 5:3), not only as a man, but a sinner. "That which is born of the flesh is flesh" (John 3:6). "Who can bring a clean thing out of an

97

unclean? Not one'' (Job 14:4). While we are Christless we are without strength (Rom. 5:6).

3. The devils have more light than men, yet are they altogether dead in sin, though they believe and tremble (Jas. 2:19), and though they confess Christ (Luke 4:34; Mark 1:24). They sin freely, yet cannot avoid it, but must sin.

Objection 2. Why is man blamed for resisting the Spirit, if no freewill? (Acts 7:51; Matt. 23:37).

Answer I. They resisted the **preaching** of the Gospel (which is the outward means of grace) by persecuting the ministers thereof. The word ''resist'' in that passage of Scripture signifies a rushing against, and falling upon in a rude and hostile manner, and fitly expresses their ill-treatment of Christ and His ministers by falling upon them and putting them to death. That is the resistance here particularly designed; see the following verse, 52. The inward work of the Spirit cannot be resisted; as the creature can neither hinder nor further his own creation, nor the dead their own resurrection, so neither can fallen man hinder or further his conversion.

2. Matt. 23:37. This scripture, so common in the mouths and so frequently found in the writings of Arminians, so readily produced by them on almost every occasion against the doctrines of grace—this scripture, taken in its context, will advantage them nothing. ''How often

98

would I have gathered," etc., "but ye would not." This gathering does not design a gathering of Jews to Christ internally, by the Spirit and grace of God; but a gathering of them externally, to hear Him preach, so that they might be brought to an assent unto Him **as the Messiah.**

This reception of Christ would not have been saving faith, but it would have preserved them from that **temporal ruin** threatened in thee following verse. This scripture therefore (as Acts 7:51) only respects a resistance to Christ's outward ministry. Jerusalem, i.e., her rulers, received Him not (John 7:48), therefore their house is to be desolated (v. 38); the city is one thing and her children another. Here is temporal destruction threatened for neglecting temporal visitations (Luke 19:44). Nationally considered, Jerusalem would have been preserved in its peace had the people, upon the rational opportunity afforded them for receiving the Messiah, accepted Christ under that character.

Objection 3. Why doth God say, "What could I do more to My vineyard?" (Isa. 5:4).

Answer I. This is not spoken of grace, that God gives to particular men peculiarly; but of great things done for Israel as a nation (Psa. 143:20). God dealt not so with other nations. "These words are part of a parable, representing the state and condition of the people of the Jews; and the design thereof is to show the ingratitude of the Jews in the midst of many favors bestowed on them, and the patience and long-suffering of God towards them, and to vindicate His justice in their ruin as a nation'' (Dr. John Gill).

2. God did enough in making man upright, and if he hath lost his uprightness, he must thank himself, and not blame God, who is not bound to restore it. Grace is the Lord's own; He giveth it to whom He will.

Objection 4. Man is a rational creature; his will cannot be determined by anything from without, it being a self-determining principle.

Answer I. Irresistible grace takes not away that natural liberty which the will hath by creation, but the depravity of it only; knocking off its fetters, but not destroying its nature. We never enjoy our will so much as when God's will overrules ours. If man can determine his own will, and destroy the liberty of it, then much more God who is the maker thereof.

2. To will is from nature, to will well is from grace; spiritual fruit must spring from a spiritual root.

"Not all the outward forms on earth,
Nor rites that God hath given,
Not will of man, nor blood, nor birth,
Can raise a soul to heaven.

The sovereign will of God alone,
Creates us heirs of grace;
Both in the image of His Son,
A new peculiar race.

Thus quicken'd souls awake and rise
From the long sleep of death;
On heavenly things they fix their eyes,
And praise employs their breath.''

CHAPTER IV.
OF FINAL PERSEVERANCE

The fifth and last point of Arminianism implies that saving grace is not an abiding principle, but that those who are loved of God, ransomed by Christ, and born again of the Spirit, may (let God wish and strive ever so much to the contrary) throw all away, and perish eternally at last.

The doctrine of the perseverance of the saints will therefore be considered in this last chapter; and the position to be defended is: That true and saving grace cannot be totally and finally lost.

For the better understanding of this I shall enquire: First, What is saving grace? Second, What is it to fall totally and finally? Third, What arguments can be assigned, or reasons given, to evidence that this special saving grace cannot be totally and finally lost?

First Inquiry. What is saving grace?

Answer. First, **negatively**. It is not the grace of nature or natural grace, which is two-fold. 1. In the pure estate. The gift of original knowledge and righteousness which was infused into the soul so soon as it had its being in pure nature. 2. In the fallen estate. The Gentiles do by nature the things contained in the law; their conscience bearing them witness, and their thoughts accusing or excusing them, according as they do well or ill (see Rom. 2:14, 15).

2. Neither is it supernatural common grace, which is called supernatural, as not attainable by the power of nature or freewill; and common, because given both to the elect and non-elect. As dexterity in callings, given by the Spirit to Bezaleel and Aholiab: "I have filled him with the Spirit of God, in wisdom, and in understanding, and in knowledge, and in all manner of workmanship" etc. (Ex. 31:2-6). Ministerial gifts, whereof Judas was a partaker. Delight in hearing the Word, as the stony ground hearer (Matt. 13:20); and Herod also, who did many things, and who heard John preach gladly (Mark 6:20). These tastes of heavenly things are given to servants as well as to sons, and differ from **saving** grace in its subject, original, efficacy, property, duration, event, and final issue.

1. In its subject; saving grace being peculiar to the elect only, and is no wider than election itself.

2. In its original; common grace flows from Christ as a Redeemer, but not as their Redeemer; and from the Spirit of Christ assisting but not as indwelling.

3. In its efficacy. Common grace may qualify for a common profession only, where there is a "form of knowledge" (Rom. 2:20), and a "form of godliness" (2 Tim. 3:5), which doth neither

renew the heart, nor raise it above a common frame, yet may do much for God (with the stony ground) and suffer much for God (with the thorny ground) and yet not be special grace "which the world cannot receive" (John 14:17), and which lives, revives and reigns, so that sin cannot have dominion (Rom. 6:14). Gifts are but as dead graces, but graces are living gifts.

4.   In its property or nature; common grace is but the ornament, not the substance of a Christian; gifts, indeed, may beautify grace, but grace only sanctifies gifts, as the gold beautified the temple, but it was the temple that sanctified the gold (Matt. 27:17). For the eminency of gifts, and the prevalency of sin, a form of godliness and the power of sin may dwell and consist together.

5.   In its duration. We acknowledge common grace may wither away; it is not a gift that God repents not of, as that gift of effectual calling is (Rom. 11:29). The greatest flood of spiritual gifts may decay to less than a drop, whereas the least drop of saving grace shall increase to a river. Thus the Spirit (in gifts of prowess and government) departed from Saul (I Sam. 16:14), and ministerial gifts (as the right arm and right eye, Zech. 11:17) may fail and be withered up.

6.   In its event and final issue. Common grace aggravates condemnation. As a sinking ship, the more it is laden with gold the deeper it

sinks; so men, the more they are laden with gifts without grace the deeper they sink into hell. As a harlot may have children but no credit or comfort from them, because they are bastards; so bastard graces, such as false hope, faith, love, etc. (if we are not one with Christ, and married to Him) never end in joy. We may bless ourselves with thoughts of embracing beautiful Rachal (as Jacob did) when in the morning of the resurrection it proves but blear-eyed Leah.

But thirdly, and now **positively,** supernatural saving grace is the sanctification of the Spirit, renewing in us the image of God, and guiding and strengthening us to obedience, and in obedience even to the end. It is His almighty effectual working on the hearts of the elect, giving to them a certain continued connection of all spiritual blessings, which manages them onward even to a state of glory. "Whom He did predestinate, them He also **called;** and whom He called, them He also justified; and whom He justified, them He also **glorified**" (Rom. 8:30). He "hath made us meet to be partakers of the inheritance of the saints in light" (Col. 1:12). The effects of it doth accompany salvation, being permanent effects; both on the soul in justification and adoption, and in the soul in vocation, sanctification, and perseverance to glorification. This grace differs not from glory in kind, but only in degree; grace is glory militant, as glory is grace triumphant. Therefore it is called "the riches of His grace" (Eph. 1:7), and "the riches of His glory" (Rom. 9:23). This is that grace which cannot be totally and finally lost. "The water that I shall give him shall be in him a well of water, springing up into everlasting life" (John 4:14).

Second Inquiry. What is it to fall totally and finally?

Answer I. To fall totally is to have grace altogether dead in us, both in the act and in the habit; no life either in branches, bole, or root; no seed remaining in us, neither any root of the matter.

2. Finally to fall is never to rise again, never to recover by repentance; but to die in sin unrepented of and unpardoned.

Third Inquiry. What scriptural arguments can be assigned, or reasons given, to evidence that this special saving grace cannot be totally and finally lost?

Answer. The following are the arguments and reasons assigned why the chosen of God cannot totally and finally fall away from grace.

Argument is taken from God the Father in His electing love. If the love of the Father to His chosen ones is an unchangeable love (Jer. 33:3); if with Him is no variableness, neither shadow of turning, (Jas. 1:17); if none can pluck out of the Father's hand (John 10:29), then His chosen ones cannot totally and finally fall away.

Neither the force nor fraud of hell can prevail against the Father's electing love, which runs parallel with eternity. "God is love" (I John 4:8), the everlasting love must needs flow from an everlasting God. He looketh on His, and saith unto them, "Yea, I have loved thee with an everlasting love" and, therefore, as the effect thereof, "I have drawn thee with the cords of loving kindness" (Jer. 31:3). It is to be declared of and from the Lord unto the Church, that "The lord thy God in the midst of thee is mighty; He will save, He will rejoice over thee with joy; He will rest in His love, He will joy over thee with singing" (Zeph. 3:17). Hence Paul, having spoken of some apostates falling away, comforts the minds of believers, saying, that their standing is firm, because of election, or rather because of electing love (2 Tim. 2:19). This he compares to a foundation and a seal, two things of the greatest validity and security. Believers stand as upon a stable rock, and they are placed as upon a mountain of brass, so cannot totally and finally fall; for the Father is not inconstant in His love; He doth not love to-day and hate to-morrow.

2.   The second argument is taken from God the Son in His redeeming love, which is unalterable.

Thereby are all the members of Christ united

unto their Head. Neither principalities nor powers shall be able to separate them from the love of God in Christ (Rom. 8:38). And the gates of hell cannot prevail against His Church (Matt. 16:18). If one member may be broken off from Christ, than all may; one having no more privilege than another in respect of their state and standing; so Christ may be supposed, upon this hypothesis, to be a head without a body or members and to have died in vain; both which are grossly absurd. Christ prayed for perseverance for His; that Peter's faith should not fail (Luke 22:32), and that His disciples should be kept from evil (John 17:15), yea, and all believers (v. 20), and what Christ prays for He is always heard therein (John 11:41,42). Christ also promises perseverance to His. "All that the Father giveth Me shall come to Me" (John 6:37). He will not utterly withdraw His mercy from them under their severest correction (Psa. 89:31-33). "Having loved His own which were in the world, He loveth them unto the end" (John 13:1), and loses not one of them (John 6:39). He is a Saviour to all parts of the body (Eph. 6:23). Saints are in Christ's hands (Deut. 33:3), and it is as easy to pluck a star out of heaven as a saint out of Christ's hands (John 10:28); they are all, and they shall all be kept by the power of God, through faith, unto eternal salvation. "Sanctified (set apart) by God the Father, preserved in

Jesus Christ, and called" (Jude 1; I Peter 1:5).

3. The third argument is taken from God the Holy Ghost, in His sanctification love. If the operation of the Spirit on the hearts of believers be a sure and certain operation, then true believers cannot totally and finally fall away.

The truth of this will appear in that the Spirit's operation is compared in Scripture; 1. To an earnest. 2. To a seal. 3. To a witness.

First, to an earnest. "God hath given unto us the earnest of the Spirit" (2 Cor. 5:5). It is the earnest penny of our salvation, not the pawn or pledge, which is to be returned again. The earnest is a part of the bargain, and the first fruits of heaven; now the earnest would be lost if the bargain of salvation stand not, and he that hath the earnest be not saved; and if such a one be damned, he carries the earnest of the Spirit along with him into hell, which must needs be absurd.

"But Christ's to the end shall endure,
As sure as the earnest is given;
More happy, but not more secure,
The glorified spirits in heaven."

Secondly, to a seal. Faith is our seal; assurance of faith is God's seal. He that believeth hath set to his seal that God is true (John 3:33). "After that ye believed ye were sealed" (Eph. 1:13). They first believed and then were sealed, i. e., fully assured. God honours our sealing to His truth by His sealing with His Spirit; as the earnest makes the bargain, so the seal ratifies and confirms it. And the broad seal of heaven must needs be more unalterable than that of the Medes and Persians.

Thirdly, to a witness. "He that believeth hath the witness in himself" (I John 5:10). And there can be no exceptions taken to this witness who abides for ever in the elect, and is called the Spirit of truth (John 14:17), which "teacheth you all things, and is truth, and is no lie" (I John 2:27); even the eternal Spirit (Heb. 9:14), a witness that can neither die nor lie. So that believers, whose bodies are called "the temple of the Holy Ghost" (I Cor. 6:19), may not become a habitation of devils. This would make Satan rejoice and insult over God (as if stronger than He) could he so dispossess Him, as he is dispossessed by Him (Luke 11:21,22).

4.   The fourth argument in defense of final perseverance respects spiritual enemies. If no spiritual enemy can prevail against a true believer totally and finally, then a true believer cannot totally and finally fall away.

1st. **Satan** cannot; for that wicked one cannot touch them with any of his deadly touches (I John 5:18), but God treads him under their feet (Rom. 16:20). The seed of the serpent may nibble at the heels of the seed of the woman, but cannot mortally wound the heart; for his armour is taken away (Luke 11:21), and his works are destroyed (Heb. 2:14). Christ in them, the hope of glory, is stronger than he that is in the world (I John 4:4).

2nd. The **world** cannot; for Christ gives them faith to conquer the world (I John 5:4), yea, He Himself has overcome the world for them (John 16:33). He makes them to be higher-region men, above all storms (Prov. 15:24); they are made kings unto God; they have a royal spirit to live above the frown and flatteries of the world; and the world, even all sublunary things, are beneath them under their feet.

3rd. Their **fleshly lusts** cannot; which have not dominion over those that are under grace (Rom. 6:14). Though all real Shulamites find the presence of the two armies (Sol. Song 6:13), the flesh lusting against the Spirit, and the Spirit against the flesh (Gal. 5:17), so that they cannot be as they would; yet the issue of the contest is not doubtful. A troop may for a time overcome Gad; coming upon him like bees (as David's phrase is, Psa. 118:12), yet Gad shall overcome at the last (Gen. 46:19). Believers are more than conquerors, even triumphers, over all their spiritual enemies, through Christ which loveth them; and no created power can prevail against them (Rom. 8:35-40). Then "thanks be unto

God, which always causeth us to triumph in Christ'' (2 Cor. 2:14).

5. Then nature of saintship proves final perseverance; if saintship be a service, subjection, sonship and marriage, then saints cannot fall away totally and finally.

1st. It is a **service**. The service of God transcends all other services; men take a servant for a year, and an apprentice for seven years, but our heavenly master for life; we are to serve God in holiness and righteousness all the days of our lives (Luke 1:74-75). A servant of God is like the Jewish servant that was bored through the ear, in token of perpetual servitude (Deut. 15:17). Religion is a perpetual obligation.

2nd. It is a **subjection**. It sets up God to be our King, and our allegiance is for life; it cannot be disclaimed (Luke 19:27). Born of God by the grace of God; and, if we be born subjects into the kingdom of this gracious Lord and King, we must die His subjects; there is no alienation.

3rd. It is a **sonship**. And this goes beyond the two former similitudes; a servant may be at liberty when his time is expired; a subject may change his earthly sovereign by removing out of his native country; yet a son cannot change his father, and he abides in the house for ever (John 8:35). Now as God hath begotten us of His own will by the Spirit of regeneration; causing us to come to Him with weeping, and leading us with supplications, because He is our Father (Jer. 31:9), and because of the relationship subsisting between Him and us He makes known His Abba love to our souls (Gal. 3:26). Therefore shall we persevere; God is our Father, and we are called the children of God.

4th. It is a **marriage state,** and that is for life too (Hosea 2:19; Isa. 54:5; Rev. 19:7; Rom. 7:1-4), and in this state God hates putting away (Mal. 2:16).

6. In respect to the saints themselves. If the names of the saints are written in heaven; if they are kept for heaven, as heaven is kept for them; and if they are compared to things that neither fade nor fail, then they cannot totally and finally fall.

1st. Their names are written in heaven (Phil. 4:3; Dan. 12:1). "Rejoice because your names are written in heaven" (Luke 10:20). To be enrolled in the book of life must needs hold **our** perseverance, for there is no blotting or blurring of that book; Satan cannot, for it is above his reach; and God will not, for then his work would not be perfect and glorious if it admitted of blottings.

2nd. Saints are kept as in a double garrison, or as with a guard; heaven for them, and they for heaven; they are kept by the power of God through faith unto salvation (I Pet. 1:4,5). Christ is their Lord, keeper, and if God had intended the loss of one saint, He would not have invested Christ with all power in heaven and earth to undertake for His children, and to save them to the very uttermost (Matt. 11:27; Heb. 7:25).

3rd. Saints are compared to a tree that fades not (Psa. 1:3); to a cedar in Lebanon (Psa. 92:12; Hosea 14:5); to Mount Zion that cannot be moved but abideth for ever (Psa. 125:1); and to a house built on a rock (Matt. 7:24). Though they fall, God raises them up (Psa. 37:24; Prov. 24:16). The Lord is with them in their old age (Isa. 46:4), and is their guide even unto death (Psa. 48:14), so that they cannot totally and finally be lost.

7. The final perseverance of the saints may be argued, seventhly, from the unchangeableness of the covenant of grace.

That which stands upon two unchangeable persons, and ratified before an unchangeable witness, must be itself unchangeable, and the covenant of grace is so.

First. It stands upon two unchangeable bottoms, even the Word and oath of God. When God made promise to Abraham, He sware by Himself, He being "willing more abundantly to show unto the heirs of promise the immutability of His counsel, confirmed it by an oath" that "we might have a strong consolation" (Heb. 1:17, 18). God's Word is as gold purified, which loses nothing of its weight, though cast a thousand times into the fire. We commonly say that the bare word of an honest man is as good as a bon; how much more the Word of the God of truth that cannot lie? And this Word is confirmed with an oath, when God swears by His holiness that He will not alter the thing that is gone out of His lips.

Secondly. It is made between two unchangeable persons (Mal. 3:6; Heb. 13:8). In this covenant there is a mutual stipulation. The Father, in covenant, gave to Christ a people (John 17:6, 9:12, 24). The Son confederates to take man's nature upon Him in the fulness of time; and in that nature to obey, magnify, and make honourable the law, and to answer the demands of Justice in our room and stead, by shedding of His own most precious blood (Psa. 40:6,7; Heb. 10:5-7; Eph. 5:26, 27). Hence it is called the blood of the everlasting covenant (Heb. 13:20).

Thirdly. It is ratified before an unchangeable witness, even the Holy Ghost. Indeed the Father and the Son, are their own Witnesses (John 5:32, 36, 37), yet the Holy Ghost is the Witness of that covenant, agreement and stipulation which was between them; as Christ hath a greater witness than that of man, so hath the covenant also, even the witness of the eternal Spirit. Thus the covenant is called "everlasting" (Heb. 13:20;

Isa. 54:8, 10; Jer. 37:38, 40), and "the sure mercies of David" (Isa. 50:3). Sure on God's part, who cannot fail in His good will to the elect, and sure also on their part, who shall have no will to depart from God. The latter is equally convenanted for with the former; therefore though the covenant permits a fall, yet it always ensures repentance after the fall, as in David and Peter, etc. The covenant doth absolutely promise the grace of perseverance, and all things that accompany salvation to the elect, even to the end of their lives.

8.   If saving grace be of a permanent nature, and not subject to corruption, then the elect cannot fall from it totally and finally.

Saving grace is called a "seed" remaining in those that are born of God (I John 3:9), an "incorruptible seed" (I Peter 1:23). Grace never differs from itself, though a gracious man doth from himself. Saving grace cannot be lost, though as respects its acts and operations it may not always be in exercise; but degrees and measures of grace (formerly attained to) may be lost. "Thou hast left thy first love" (Rev. 2:4), not the habit, neither wholly the exercise of love, but only that vigor and heat that once appeared.

9.   The Israelites, who were a type of God's spiritual Israel, could not alienate their inheritance in the land of promise (Lev. 25:23, 24; I Kings 21;3); if this was so in the type, then

must it hold true also in the anti-type.

A true Christian cannot alienate his inheritance in heaven, for the deeds concerning this inheritance are written and sealed, and part possession is given the believer even in this life (Jer. 32:40). "I will put My fear in their hearts [present gracious possession] that they shall not depart from Me" [perseverance to glorification]. Christ is able to keep the deposit committed unto Him against that day (2 Tim. 1:12). He is not only our goal, our near Kinsman, who has redeemed our mortgaged inheritance for us; but He is our officer in trust also, keeping heaven for us and us for heaven; and He abideth faithful (2 Tim. 2:13), both in drawing, that we should come to Him, and in holding, that we should not depart from Him. Even now is He sealed at the right hand of the Father, interceding on our behalf, and saying, "Father, I will that they also whom Thou hast given Me, be with me where I am; that they may behold My glory, which Thou hast given Me" (John 17:24).

> "His powerful blood did once atone,
> And now it pleads before the throne."

10. If those that fall totally and finally be not (nor ever were) true believers, then it follows that such as are true believers cannot do so.

The truth of this appears from John 8:31; those only are Christ's disciples which continue in His word; and such as wholly fall away have but the flashing of a temporary faith, which, like a land flood, fills the country with inundations, yet at last comes to nothing. "They went out from us because they were not of us" (I John 2:19). All true believers continue to the end (Heb. 3:6,14); those are God's house and partakers of Christ indeed, and those only.

11.　The eleventh argument is taken from the subject of prayer.

Whatsoever true believers ask of the Father in the name of Christ, according to His will, shall assuredly be obtained (John 14:13, 14; I John 5;14, 15); and they pray for grace of perseverance. The church is represented as coming up from the wilderness, leaning on her beloved (Sol. Song 8:5); convinced of her own weakness, she leaneth on the Strength of Israel (Psa. 84:5) "Hold Thou me up, and I shall be safe" (Psa. 119:117). "My soul cleaveth to the dust: quicken Thou me" (Psa. 119:25). "I am Thine, save me" (Psa. 119:94)—cause me to persevere. These are the petitions of the believing soul, who is convinced that his strength is perfect in weakness, his wisdom is folly in the abstract, and that he is not safe from falling one moment but as supported by the arm of Omnipotence. Believers pray for perseverance, and it is said that they never seek the Lord in vain (Isa. 45:19).

12. The last argument for the final perseverance of the saints is taken from the whole concurrent voice of Scripture testimony. "The word of the Lord shall stand for ever" (Isa. 40:8).

Dr. Moulin and others have computed the texts of Scripture, which declare the doctrine of the saints' final perseverance, at six hundred; the twelve following may, however, suffice (merely as a sample) to establish it as a gospel truth: Rom. 11:29; John 10:28,29; Luke 22:32; Rom. 8:30,38, 40; I John 2:19, 27; 2 Cor. 1:21,22; Phil. 1:6; 2 Tim. 2:19; Mal. 3:6; John 14:19; Jer. 32:40; I Peter 1:3,4,5.

"The Mount Zion of the Lord (Psa. 125) is immoveable. They cannot be removed from the love of God, in which they are rooted and grounded; nor from out of the covenant of grace; nor out of the hands of Christ, out of whose hands none can pluck them; nor can they be removed off Christ, the foundation on which they are laid, which is a sure and an everlasting foundation; nor out of a state of grace in which they stand; neither out of sanctification, which is connected with life everlasting; nor yet of justification, for those who have passed from death unto life shall never enter into condemnation. These, like Mount Zion, abide forever. They abide on the heart of God, and in the hands of Christ; they abide in the house of God, and among the family of His people. The Lord surrounds them with His love, encompasses them with His favors, guards them by His special providence, watches over them night and day, and keeps them by His power (as in a garrison) through faith unto salvation.'' (Dr. John Gill).

Now if all these things are true, as they most certainly are, **then shall the whole Church finally persevere in grace, and be eternally saved.**

"How oft have sin and Satan strove
To rend my soul from Thee, my God,
But everlasting is Thy love,
And Jesus seals it with His blood, Hallelujah.''

The gospel bears my spirit up;
A faithful and unchanging God
Lays the foundation of my hope,
In oaths, and promises, and blood. Hallelujah.''

Objections Against the Doctrine of Final Perseverance Answered

Objection I. To teach that grace cannot be lost will beget looseness in professors.

Answer I. Ah! this is but the state cry of old carnality against the doctrines of grace, viz., that they lead to licentiousness. Swine may trample pearls under their feet (Matt. 7:6). Ungodly men may and do turn the grace of our God into lasciviousness (Jude 4). Head-knowledge of gospel truths and holy doctrines (the man being destitute of heart experience, and a stranger to the Spirit's work) will never bring forth fruit unto God. It is in the nature of fallen man to love sin. "He drinketh iniquity like water" (Job 15:16); and it is the work of the Spirit to convince of sin, even of its exceeding sinfulness; without this conviction, no hatred of sin, no love of holiness, whatever the outward profession may be. Satan is glad to see carnal persons professing religion; they are sure (sooner or later) to disgrace that profession, and then the doctrines of grace are charged with being the cause thereof; whereas they have a direct contrary tendency, even "teaching us that, denying ungodliness and worldly lusts, we should live soberly, righteously, and godly in this present world" (Tit. 2:12). The two seeds are minutely described by their fruits in I John 3:8-10.

2. Grace may be considered in the being, or well-being thereof. It is, first, radical and fundamental, tending to the being of a saint, as faith, hope, and love; and second, flowing from these for his well-being only, as joy of faith, confidence of hope, zeal and fervency of love; these are the lustre and radiancy of the radical principle; the beams of the sun, as those the sap and substance. The latter we may lose, and perhaps irrecoverably (Psa. 51:12); not so the former. The root remains, though reins be consumed (Job 19:27, 28); it is "a well of water springing up to everlasting life" (John 4:14 and 7:38).

3. There is a Divine purpose to be holy even to the end. This is a law written in every renewed will. There is also a Divine performance or prosecution of this purpose. This is not always found alike active in a gracious heart. This ebbs and flows according to the Spirit's influence upon us. "How to perform that which is good I find not" (Rom. 7:18). Our life is not hid in ourselves, but it is "hid with Christ in God" (Col. 3:3), and this requires our daily dependence on His Spirit (Phil. 2:13, and 4:13). In the practical part, a partial decay may befall our judgements, as in the bewitched Galatians (Gal. 3:1), and our affections may cool, as in the Ephesian Church (Rev. 2:4). Christ's "spouse" may be in a drowsy frame, yet her heart awakes (Sol. Song 5:2). Grace may, at times, seem to be lost to a child of God when it is indeed not so. The sun may be eclipsed, yet regain his former lustre; the tree may lose all its fruit and leaves in winter, yet have fresh buddings at spring; Israel flies once, yea twice before her enemies, yet conquer they the land of promise. A troop overcomes Gad, yet Gad overcomes at last. And wherefore all this? "Because I live, ye shall live also" (John 14:19).

4. Although all the sins of God's people were imputed to Christ, "The Lord hath laid on Him the iniquity of us all" (Isa. 53:6); and although the blood of Christ has cleansed, and an application thereof by the Spirit continues to

cleanse from all sin (John 1:29); yet sin still is, what it ever was, exceedingly sinful. And if one sinful thought remains unatoned for by Christ (on behalf of His people), there is evil enough in it to sink to the lowest hell. Though God doth not disinherit us for sin, neither blot us out of the book of life, yet doth He, when we sin against Him, withdraw His favour, and embitter all our comforts. He makes relations (that should be comforts) to become scourges to us (2 Sam. 12:11), and fill us with anguish (Psa. 38:3). Surely many of the children of God have found that the evil they have smarted under for sin, after sin hath been committed, has been fully commensurate to all the pleasure found in that sin. Could David have forseen the evil consequences of his sin (in the matter of Uriah's wife), he might have said, "A dear-bought sin thou art like to be to me." Yea, sometimes God may add apprehensions of eternal wrath for sin, without any hope of deliverance (Psa. 88:6,7). As the covenant Father of His covenant children, their transgressions He visits with the rod, and their iniquity with stripes; nevertheless, His loving-kindness is not removed, neither is His faithfulness suffered to fail (Psa. 89:32, 33). Upon these considerations the doctrine of final perseverance begets no looseness in those who are possessors of the grace of the doctrine, whatever it may in those who are professors only.

Objection 2. It is said of some that they made shipwreck of faith (I Tim. 1:19), and a falling from grace may be proved from Heb. 6:5, etc.

Answer I. It will be granted that to make shipwreck of faith, so as to blaspheme the doctrines of the Gospel which persons once professed, is to fall from the profession of the faith; but then, to fall from doctrine of the Gospel and a profession thereof, and to fall from the grace and favour of God, or from the grace of faith, are very different things indeed. The reasons assigned for making shipwreck of faith are shown in I John 2:19. The stony ground hearers endure "but a while," having no root (Matt. 13:21); by and by they are offended, fall away, and are said to give up, or make shipwreck of that which they never possessed but in appearance (Luke 8:18). While some are savingly enlightened by the Spirit of God to see their lost state and condition, their need of salvation by Christ and their interest therein, who shall never perish; there are others who are enlightened only into the scheme of the doctrines of the Gospel; and some of these persons to such a degree as to be able to preach them to others, and yet are themselves entirely destitute of the grace of God. When such fall away, they are no proofs nor instances of the final apostasy of real saints.

2.   It is spoken also in Heb. 6:5 of such as only taste, but digest not; that have their minds in-

formed, not their hearts reformed; sanctified in profession, not in power. And the apostle was persuaded otherwise of these Hebrews to whom he wrote; he was convinced that their faith was not an historical one, but of the operation of God (Col. 2:12), evidenced by their fruits, (vv. 9, 10; I Thess. 1:5).

3. Objections may be multiplied by the impugners of the doctrines of grace, and very conclusive and scriptural replies made thereto; yet, as concerns the final perseverance of true saints, of the Father's beloved sones, the Son's redeemed ones, and the Spirit's sanctified ones, as Christ once dead dies no more, so in His members the life of grace cannot die totally (Rom. 6:8,9). Faith is given once to the saints; as we are born but once, so but once again. "This is the Father's will which hath sent Me, that of all which He hath given Me I should lose **nothing** . . . that every one which seeth the Son, and believeth on Him, may have **everlasting** life: and I will raise him up at the last day" (John 6:39, 40).

"Not as the world, the Saviour gives:
He is no fickle friend;
Whom once He loves, He never leaves,
But loves him to the end.

Though thousand snares enclose his feet,
Not one shall hold him fast;
Whatever dangers he may meet,
He shall get safe at last.

125

The spirit that would this truth withstand
    Would pull God's temple down,
  Wrest Jesus' sceptre from His hand,
    And spoil Him of his crown.

  Satan might then full victory boast,
    The Church might wholly fall;
    If one believer may be lost,
      It follows, so may all.

But Christ, in every age, has prov'd,
    His purchase firm and true;
  If this foundation be removed,
    What shall the righteous do?''